STORYBOARD

NOTEBOOK

_____

Name

_____

Phone

_____

Email

NOTES:

_____

_____

_____

_____

_____

_____

_____

_____

_____

_____

_____

_____

_____

_____

_____

_____

FEATURES:

- 8.25 x 6 in Landscape Pages
- 6 Panel Blank Storyboard Layout
- 16:9 Aspect Ratio
- Space for Description/Dialogue and Audio
- 250 Numbered Storyboard Pages
- Table of Contents

Storyboard Notebook: 8.25 x 6 in,
6 Panel 16:9, 250 Pages, Black and Gold Theme

ISBN: 9781793254849

Copyright © 2019
GOLDING NOTEBOOKS

Printed in the USA

See the wide-ranging collection of
GOLDING NOTEBOOKS
now available on Amazon.

TABLE OF CONTENTS

Page No.	Title

Page No.	Title

TABLE OF CONTENTS

Page No.	Title

Page No.	Title

Scene:

Shot: Duration:

Description/Dialogue: _____

_____

Audio: _____

Scene:

Shot: Duration:

Description/Dialogue: _____

_____

Audio: _____

Scene:

Shot: Duration:

Description/Dialogue: _____

_____

Audio: _____

Scene:

Shot: Duration:

Description/Dialogue: _____

_____

Audio: _____

Scene:

Shot: Duration:

Description/Dialogue: _____

_____

Audio: _____

Scene:

Shot: Duration:

Description/Dialogue: _____

_____

Audio: _____

Scene:

Shot: Duration:

Description/Dialogue: _____

_____

Audio: _____

Scene:

Shot: Duration:

Description/Dialogue: _____

_____

Audio: _____

Scene:

Shot: Duration:

Description/Dialogue: _____

_____

Audio: _____

Scene:

Shot: Duration:

Description/Dialogue: _____

_____

Audio: _____

Scene:

Shot: Duration:

Description/Dialogue: _____

_____

Audio: _____

Scene:

Shot: Duration:

Description/Dialogue: _____

_____

Audio: _____

Scene:

Shot:　　　　　　　　　Duration:

Description/Dialogue: _____

Audio: _____

Scene:

Shot:　　　　　　　　　Duration:

Description/Dialogue: _____

Audio: _____

Scene:

Shot:　　　　　　　　　Duration:

Description/Dialogue: _____

Audio: _____

Scene:

Shot:　　　　　　　　　Duration:

Description/Dialogue: _____

Audio: _____

Scene:

Shot:　　　　　　　　　Duration:

Description/Dialogue: _____

Audio: _____

Scene:

Shot:　　　　　　　　　Duration:

Description/Dialogue: _____

Audio: _____

Scene:

Shot: Duration:

Description/Dialogue: —————————————

Audio: —————

Scene:

Shot: Duration:

Description/Dialogue: —————————————

Audio: —————

Scene:

Shot: Duration:

Description/Dialogue: —————————————

Audio: —————

Scene:

Shot: Duration:

Description/Dialogue: —————————————

Audio: —————

Scene:

Shot: Duration:

Description/Dialogue: —————————————

Audio: —————

Scene:

Shot: Duration:

Description/Dialogue: —————————————

Audio: —————

Scene:

Shot: Duration:

Description/Dialogue: _____

_____

Audio: _____

Scene:

Shot: Duration:

Description/Dialogue: _____

_____

Audio: _____

Scene:

Shot: Duration:

Description/Dialogue: _____

_____

Audio: _____

Scene:

Shot: Duration:

Description/Dialogue: _____

_____

Audio: _____

Scene:

Shot: Duration:

Description/Dialogue: _____

_____

Audio: _____

Scene:

Shot: Duration:

Description/Dialogue: _____

_____

Audio: _____

Scene:

Shot: Duration:

Description/Dialogue: ——————————————

Audio: ————————————————————

Scene:

Shot: Duration:

Description/Dialogue: ——————————————

Audio: ————————————————————

Scene:

Shot: Duration:

Description/Dialogue: ——————————————

Audio: ————————————————————

Scene:

Shot: Duration:

Description/Dialogue: ——————————————

Audio: ————————————————————

Scene:

Shot: Duration:

Description/Dialogue: ——————————————

Audio: ————————————————————

Scene:

Shot: Duration:

Description/Dialogue: ——————————————

Audio: ————————————————————

Scene:

Shot: Duration:

Description/Dialogue:

Audio:

Scene:

Shot: Duration:

Description/Dialogue:

Audio:

Scene:

Shot: Duration:

Description/Dialogue:

Audio:

Scene:

Shot: Duration:

Description/Dialogue:

Audio:

Scene:

Shot: Duration:

Description/Dialogue:

Audio:

Scene:

Shot: Duration:

Description/Dialogue:

Audio:

Scene:

Shot: Duration:

Description/Dialogue: ⎯⎯⎯⎯⎯⎯⎯

Audio: ⎯⎯⎯⎯⎯⎯⎯

Scene:

Shot: Duration:

Description/Dialogue: ⎯⎯⎯⎯⎯⎯⎯

Audio: ⎯⎯⎯⎯⎯⎯⎯

Scene:

Shot: Duration:

Description/Dialogue: ⎯⎯⎯⎯⎯⎯⎯

Audio: ⎯⎯⎯⎯⎯⎯⎯

Scene:

Shot: Duration:

Description/Dialogue: ⎯⎯⎯⎯⎯⎯⎯

Audio: ⎯⎯⎯⎯⎯⎯⎯

Scene:

Shot: Duration:

Description/Dialogue: ⎯⎯⎯⎯⎯⎯⎯

Audio: ⎯⎯⎯⎯⎯⎯⎯

Scene:

Shot: Duration:

Description/Dialogue: ⎯⎯⎯⎯⎯⎯⎯

Audio: ⎯⎯⎯⎯⎯⎯⎯

Scene:

Shot: Duration:

Description/Dialogue: _____

Audio: _____

Scene:

Shot: Duration:

Description/Dialogue: _____

Audio: _____

Scene:

Shot: Duration:

Description/Dialogue: _____

Audio: _____

Scene:

Shot: Duration:

Description/Dialogue: _____

Audio: _____

Scene:

Shot: Duration:

Description/Dialogue: _____

Audio: _____

Scene:

Shot: Duration:

Description/Dialogue: _____

Audio: _____

Scene:

Shot: Duration:

Description/Dialogue: _____

_____

Audio: _____

Scene:

Shot: Duration:

Description/Dialogue: _____

_____

Audio: _____

Scene:

Shot: Duration:

Description/Dialogue: _____

_____

Audio: _____

Scene:

Shot: Duration:

Description/Dialogue: _____

_____

Audio: _____

Scene:

Shot: Duration:

Description/Dialogue: _____

_____

Audio: _____

Scene:

Shot: Duration:

Description/Dialogue: _____

_____

Audio: _____

Scene:

Shot: Duration:

Description/Dialogue: _____

Audio: _____

Scene:

Shot: Duration:

Description/Dialogue: _____

Audio: _____

Scene:

Shot: Duration:

Description/Dialogue: _____

Audio: _____

Scene:

Shot: Duration:

Description/Dialogue: _____

Audio: _____

Scene:

Shot: Duration:

Description/Dialogue: _____

Audio: _____

Scene:

Shot: Duration:

Description/Dialogue: _____

Audio: _____

Scene:

Shot: Duration:

Description/Dialogue: _____

Audio: _____

Scene:

Shot: Duration:

Description/Dialogue: _____

Audio: _____

Scene:

Shot: Duration:

Description/Dialogue: _____

Audio: _____

Scene:

Shot: Duration:

Description/Dialogue: _____

Audio: _____

Scene:

Shot: Duration:

Description/Dialogue: _____

Audio: _____

Scene:

Shot: Duration:

Description/Dialogue: _____

Audio: _____

Scene:

Shot: Duration:

Description/Dialogue: _____

_____

Audio: _____

Scene:

Shot: Duration:

Description/Dialogue: _____

_____

Audio: _____

Scene:

Shot: Duration:

Description/Dialogue: _____

_____

Audio: _____

Scene:

Shot: Duration:

Description/Dialogue: _____

_____

Audio: _____

Scene:

Shot: Duration:

Description/Dialogue: _____

_____

Audio: _____

Scene:

Shot: Duration:

Description/Dialogue: _____

_____

Audio: _____

Scene:

Shot: Duration:

Description/Dialogue: _____

Audio: _____

Scene:

Shot: Duration:

Description/Dialogue: _____

Audio: _____

Scene:

Shot: Duration:

Description/Dialogue: _____

Audio: _____

Scene:

Shot: Duration:

Description/Dialogue: _____

Audio: _____

Scene:

Shot: Duration:

Description/Dialogue: _____

Audio: _____

Scene:

Shot: Duration:

Description/Dialogue: _____

Audio: _____

Scene:

Shot: Duration:

Description/Dialogue:

Audio:

Scene:

Shot: Duration:

Description/Dialogue:

Audio:

Scene:

Shot: Duration:

Description/Dialogue:

Audio:

Scene:

Shot: Duration:

Description/Dialogue:

Audio:

Scene:

Shot: Duration:

Description/Dialogue:

Audio:

Scene:

Shot: Duration:

Description/Dialogue:

Audio:

Scene:

Shot: Duration:

Description/Dialogue: _____

Audio: _____

Scene:

Shot: Duration:

Description/Dialogue: _____

Audio: _____

Scene:

Shot: Duration:

Description/Dialogue: _____

Audio: _____

Scene:

Shot: Duration:

Description/Dialogue: _____

Audio: _____

Scene:

Shot: Duration:

Description/Dialogue: _____

Audio: _____

Scene:

Shot: Duration:

Description/Dialogue: _____

Audio: _____

Scene:

Shot: Duration:

Description/Dialogue:

Audio:

Scene:

Shot: Duration:

Description/Dialogue:

Audio:

Scene:

Shot: Duration:

Description/Dialogue:

Audio:

Scene:

Shot: Duration:

Description/Dialogue:

Audio:

Scene:

Shot: Duration:

Description/Dialogue:

Audio:

Scene:

Shot: Duration:

Description/Dialogue:

Audio:

Scene:

Shot: Duration:

Description/Dialogue:

Audio:

Scene:

Shot: Duration:

Description/Dialogue:

Audio:

Scene:

Shot: Duration:

Description/Dialogue:

Audio:

Scene:

Shot: Duration:

Description/Dialogue:

Audio:

Scene:

Shot: Duration:

Description/Dialogue:

Audio:

Scene:

Shot: Duration:

Description/Dialogue:

Audio:

Scene:

Shot: Duration:

Description/Dialogue: _____

Audio: _____

Scene:

Shot: Duration:

Description/Dialogue: _____

Audio: _____

Scene:

Shot: Duration:

Description/Dialogue: _____

Audio: _____

Scene:

Shot: Duration:

Description/Dialogue: _____

Audio: _____

Scene:

Shot: Duration:

Description/Dialogue: _____

Audio: _____

Scene:

Shot: Duration:

Description/Dialogue: _____

Audio: _____

Scene:

Shot: Duration:

Description/Dialogue: _____

Audio: _____

Scene:

Shot: Duration:

Description/Dialogue: _____

Audio: _____

Scene:

Shot: Duration:

Description/Dialogue: _____

Audio: _____

Scene:

Shot: Duration:

Description/Dialogue: _____

Audio: _____

Scene:

Shot: Duration:

Description/Dialogue: _____

Audio: _____

Scene:

Shot: Duration:

Description/Dialogue: _____

Audio: _____

Scene:

Shot: Duration:

Description/Dialogue: —————————————————

Audio: —————————————————

Scene:

Shot: Duration:

Description/Dialogue: —————————————————

Audio: —————————————————

Scene:

Shot: Duration:

Description/Dialogue: —————————————————

Audio: —————————————————

Scene:

Shot: Duration:

Description/Dialogue: —————————————————

Audio: —————————————————

Scene:

Shot: Duration:

Description/Dialogue: —————————————————

Audio: —————————————————

Scene:

Shot: Duration:

Description/Dialogue: —————————————————

Audio: —————————————————

Scene:

Shot: Duration:

Description/Dialogue: _____

Audio: _____

Scene:

Shot: Duration:

Description/Dialogue: _____

Audio: _____

Scene:

Shot: Duration:

Description/Dialogue: _____

Audio: _____

Scene:

Shot: Duration:

Description/Dialogue: _____

Audio: _____

Scene:

Shot: Duration:

Description/Dialogue: _____

Audio: _____

Scene:

Shot: Duration:

Description/Dialogue: _____

Audio: _____

Scene:

Shot: Duration:

Description/Dialogue: _____

Audio: _____

Scene:

Shot: Duration:

Description/Dialogue: _____

Audio: _____

Scene:

Shot: Duration:

Description/Dialogue: _____

Audio: _____

Scene:

Shot: Duration:

Description/Dialogue: _____

Audio: _____

Scene:

Shot: Duration:

Description/Dialogue: _____

Audio: _____

Scene:

Shot: Duration:

Description/Dialogue: _____

Audio: _____

Scene:

Shot: Duration:

Description/Dialogue: _____

Audio: _____

Scene:

Shot: Duration:

Description/Dialogue: _____

Audio: _____

Scene:

Shot: Duration:

Description/Dialogue: _____

Audio: _____

Scene:

Shot: Duration:

Description/Dialogue: _____

Audio: _____

Scene:

Shot: Duration:

Description/Dialogue: _____

Audio: _____

Scene:

Shot: Duration:

Description/Dialogue: _____

Audio: _____

Scene:

Shot: Duration:

Description/Dialogue: _____

_____

Audio: _____

Scene:

Shot: Duration:

Description/Dialogue: _____

_____

Audio: _____

Scene:

Shot: Duration:

Description/Dialogue: _____

_____

Audio: _____

Scene:

Shot: Duration:

Description/Dialogue: _____

_____

Audio: _____

Scene:

Shot: Duration:

Description/Dialogue: _____

_____

Audio: _____

Scene:

Shot: Duration:

Description/Dialogue: _____

_____

Audio: _____

Scene:

Shot: Duration:

Description/Dialogue: _____

_____

Audio: _____

Scene:

Shot: Duration:

Description/Dialogue: _____

_____

Audio: _____

Scene:

Shot: Duration:

Description/Dialogue: _____

_____

Audio: _____

Scene:

Shot: Duration:

Description/Dialogue: _____

_____

Audio: _____

Scene:

Shot: Duration:

Description/Dialogue: _____

_____

Audio: _____

Scene:

Shot: Duration:

Description/Dialogue: _____

_____

Audio: _____

Scene:

Shot: Duration:

Description/Dialogue: _____

Audio: _____

Scene:

Shot: Duration:

Description/Dialogue: _____

Audio: _____

Scene:

Shot: Duration:

Description/Dialogue: _____

Audio: _____

Scene:

Shot: Duration:

Description/Dialogue: _____

Audio: _____

Scene:

Shot: Duration:

Description/Dialogue: _____

Audio: _____

Scene:

Shot: Duration:

Description/Dialogue: _____

Audio: _____

Scene:

Shot: Duration:

Description/Dialogue: —————————————

Audio: ——————————————————

Scene:

Shot: Duration:

Description/Dialogue: —————————————

Audio: ——————————————————

Scene:

Shot: Duration:

Description/Dialogue: —————————————

Audio: ——————————————————

Scene:

Shot: Duration:

Description/Dialogue: —————————————

Audio: ——————————————————

Scene:

Shot: Duration:

Description/Dialogue: —————————————

Audio: ——————————————————

Scene:

Shot: Duration:

Description/Dialogue: —————————————

Audio: ——————————————————

Scene:

Shot: Duration:

Description/Dialogue: _____

_____

Audio: _____

Scene:

Shot: Duration:

Description/Dialogue: _____

_____

Audio: _____

Scene:

Shot: Duration:

Description/Dialogue: _____

_____

Audio: _____

Scene:

Shot: Duration:

Description/Dialogue: _____

_____

Audio: _____

Scene:

Shot: Duration:

Description/Dialogue: _____

_____

Audio: _____

Scene:

Shot: Duration:

Description/Dialogue: _____

_____

Audio: _____

Scene:

Shot: Duration:

Description/Dialogue: _____

_____

_____

Audio: _____

Scene:

Shot: Duration:

Description/Dialogue: _____

_____

_____

Audio: _____

Scene:

Shot: Duration:

Description/Dialogue: _____

_____

_____

Audio: _____

Scene:

Shot: Duration:

Description/Dialogue: _____

_____

_____

Audio: _____

Scene:

Shot: Duration:

Description/Dialogue: _____

_____

_____

Audio: _____

Scene:

Shot: Duration:

Description/Dialogue: _____

_____

_____

Audio: _____

Scene:

Shot: Duration:

Description/Dialogue: _____

_____

Audio: _____

Scene:

Shot: Duration:

Description/Dialogue: _____

_____

Audio: _____

Scene:

Shot: Duration:

Description/Dialogue: _____

_____

Audio: _____

Scene:

Shot: Duration:

Description/Dialogue: _____

_____

Audio: _____

Scene:

Shot: Duration:

Description/Dialogue: _____

_____

Audio: _____

Scene:

Shot: Duration:

Description/Dialogue: _____

_____

Audio: _____

Scene:

Shot: Duration:

Description/Dialogue: _____

_____

Audio: _____

Scene:

Shot: Duration:

Description/Dialogue: _____

_____

Audio: _____

Scene:

Shot: Duration:

Description/Dialogue: _____

_____

Audio: _____

Scene:

Shot: Duration:

Description/Dialogue: _____

_____

Audio: _____

Scene:

Shot: Duration:

Description/Dialogue: _____

_____

Audio: _____

Scene:

Shot: Duration:

Description/Dialogue: _____

_____

Audio: _____

Scene:

Shot: Duration:

Description/Dialogue: _____

_____

Audio: _____

Scene:

Shot: Duration:

Description/Dialogue: _____

_____

Audio: _____

Scene:

Shot: Duration:

Description/Dialogue: _____

_____

Audio: _____

Scene:

Shot: Duration:

Description/Dialogue: _____

_____

Audio: _____

Scene:

Shot: Duration:

Description/Dialogue: _____

_____

Audio: _____

Scene:

Shot: Duration:

Description/Dialogue: _____

_____

Audio: _____

Scene:

Shot: Duration:

Description/Dialogue: ——————————————

Audio: —————————————————

Scene:

Shot: Duration:

Description/Dialogue: ——————————————

Audio: —————————————————

Scene:

Shot: Duration:

Description/Dialogue: ——————————————

Audio: —————————————————

Scene:

Shot: Duration:

Description/Dialogue: ——————————————

Audio: —————————————————

Scene:

Shot: Duration:

Description/Dialogue: ——————————————

Audio: —————————————————

Scene:

Shot: Duration:

Description/Dialogue: ——————————————

Audio: —————————————————

Scene:

Shot: Duration:

Description/Dialogue:

Audio:

Scene:

Shot: Duration:

Description/Dialogue:

Audio:

Scene:

Shot: Duration:

Description/Dialogue:

Audio:

Scene:

Shot: Duration:

Description/Dialogue:

Audio:

Scene:

Shot: Duration:

Description/Dialogue:

Audio:

Scene:

Shot: Duration:

Description/Dialogue:

Audio:

Scene:

Shot: Duration:

Description/Dialogue: _____

_____

Audio: _____

Scene:

Shot: Duration:

Description/Dialogue: _____

_____

Audio: _____

Scene:

Shot: Duration:

Description/Dialogue: _____

_____

Audio: _____

Scene:

Shot: Duration:

Description/Dialogue: _____

_____

Audio: _____

Scene:

Shot: Duration:

Description/Dialogue: _____

_____

Audio: _____

Scene:

Shot: Duration:

Description/Dialogue: _____

_____

Audio: _____

Scene:

Shot: Duration:

Description/Dialogue: _____

Audio: _____

Scene:

Shot: Duration:

Description/Dialogue: _____

Audio: _____

Scene:

Shot: Duration:

Description/Dialogue: _____

Audio: _____

Scene:

Shot: Duration:

Description/Dialogue: _____

Audio: _____

Scene:

Shot: Duration:

Description/Dialogue: _____

Audio: _____

Scene:

Shot: Duration:

Description/Dialogue: _____

Audio: _____

Scene:

Shot: Duration:

Description/Dialogue: _____

_____

Audio: _____

Scene:

Shot: Duration:

Description/Dialogue: _____

_____

Audio: _____

Scene:

Shot: Duration:

Description/Dialogue: _____

_____

Audio: _____

Scene:

Shot: Duration:

Description/Dialogue: _____

_____

Audio: _____

Scene:

Shot: Duration:

Description/Dialogue: _____

_____

Audio: _____

Scene:

Shot: Duration:

Description/Dialogue: _____

_____

Audio: _____

Scene:

Shot: Duration:

Description/Dialogue: _____

Audio: _____

Scene:

Shot: Duration:

Description/Dialogue: _____

Audio: _____

Scene:

Shot: Duration:

Description/Dialogue: _____

Audio: _____

Scene:

Shot: Duration:

Description/Dialogue: _____

Audio: _____

Scene:

Shot: Duration:

Description/Dialogue: _____

Audio: _____

Scene:

Shot: Duration:

Description/Dialogue: _____

Audio: _____

Scene:

Shot: Duration:

Description/Dialogue: _____

_____

Audio: _____

Scene:

Shot: Duration:

Description/Dialogue: _____

_____

Audio: _____

Scene:

Shot: Duration:

Description/Dialogue: _____

_____

Audio: _____

Scene:

Shot: Duration:

Description/Dialogue: _____

_____

Audio: _____

Scene:

Shot: Duration:

Description/Dialogue: _____

_____

Audio: _____

Scene:

Shot: Duration:

Description/Dialogue: _____

_____

Audio: _____

Scene:

Shot: Duration:

Description/Dialogue: _____

_____

_____

Audio: _____

Scene:

Shot: Duration:

Description/Dialogue: _____

_____

_____

Audio: _____

Scene:

Shot: Duration:

Description/Dialogue: _____

_____

_____

Audio: _____

Scene:

Shot: Duration:

Description/Dialogue: _____

_____

_____

Audio: _____

Scene:

Shot: Duration:

Description/Dialogue: _____

_____

_____

Audio: _____

Scene:

Shot: Duration:

Description/Dialogue: _____

_____

_____

Audio: _____

Scene:

Shot: | Duration:

Description/Dialogue: _____

Audio: _____

Scene:

Shot: | Duration:

Description/Dialogue: _____

Audio: _____

Scene:

Shot: | Duration:

Description/Dialogue: _____

Audio: _____

Scene:

Shot: | Duration:

Description/Dialogue: _____

Audio: _____

Scene:

Shot: | Duration:

Description/Dialogue: _____

Audio: _____

Scene:

Shot: | Duration:

Description/Dialogue: _____

Audio: _____

Scene:

Shot: Duration:

Description/Dialogue: _____

Audio: _____

Scene:

Shot: Duration:

Description/Dialogue: _____

Audio: _____

Scene:

Shot: Duration:

Description/Dialogue: _____

Audio: _____

Scene:

Shot: Duration:

Description/Dialogue: _____

Audio: _____

Scene:

Shot: Duration:

Description/Dialogue: _____

Audio: _____

Scene:

Shot: Duration:

Description/Dialogue: _____

Audio: _____

Scene:

Shot: Duration:

Description/Dialogue: ——————————————

——————————————————————

Audio: ————————————————————

Scene:

Shot: Duration:

Description/Dialogue: ——————————————

——————————————————————

Audio: ————————————————————

Scene:

Shot: Duration:

Description/Dialogue: ——————————————

——————————————————————

Audio: ————————————————————

Scene:

Shot: Duration:

Description/Dialogue: ——————————————

——————————————————————

Audio: ————————————————————

Scene:

Shot: Duration:

Description/Dialogue: ——————————————

——————————————————————

Audio: ————————————————————

Scene:

Shot: Duration:

Description/Dialogue: ——————————————

——————————————————————

Audio: ————————————————————

Scene:

Shot: Duration:

Description/Dialogue: _____

_____

Audio: _____

Scene:

Shot: Duration:

Description/Dialogue: _____

_____

Audio: _____

Scene:

Shot: Duration:

Description/Dialogue: _____

_____

Audio: _____

Scene:

Shot: Duration:

Description/Dialogue: _____

_____

Audio: _____

Scene:

Shot: Duration:

Description/Dialogue: _____

_____

Audio: _____

Scene:

Shot: Duration:

Description/Dialogue: _____

_____

Audio: _____

Scene:

Shot: Duration:

Description/Dialogue: ———————————

Audio: ————————————

Scene:

Shot: Duration:

Description/Dialogue: ———————————

Audio: ————————————

Scene:

Shot: Duration:

Description/Dialogue: ———————————

Audio: ————————————

Scene:

Shot: Duration:

Description/Dialogue: ———————————

Audio: ————————————

Scene:

Shot: Duration:

Description/Dialogue: ———————————

Audio: ————————————

Scene:

Shot: Duration:

Description/Dialogue: ———————————

Audio: ————————————

Scene:

Shot: Duration:

Description/Dialogue: _____

_____

Audio: _____

Scene:

Shot: Duration:

Description/Dialogue: _____

_____

Audio: _____

Scene:

Shot: Duration:

Description/Dialogue: _____

_____

Audio: _____

Scene:

Shot: Duration:

Description/Dialogue: _____

_____

Audio: _____

Scene:

Shot: Duration:

Description/Dialogue: _____

_____

Audio: _____

Scene:

Shot: Duration:

Description/Dialogue: _____

_____

Audio: _____

Scene:

Shot: Duration:

Description/Dialogue: —————————————

Audio: —————————————————

Scene:

Shot: Duration:

Description/Dialogue: —————————————

Audio: —————————————————

Scene:

Shot: Duration:

Description/Dialogue: —————————————

Audio: —————————————————

Scene:

Shot: Duration:

Description/Dialogue: —————————————

Audio: —————————————————

Scene:

Shot: Duration:

Description/Dialogue: —————————————

Audio: —————————————————

Scene:

Shot: Duration:

Description/Dialogue: —————————————

Audio: —————————————————

Scene:

Shot: Duration:

Description/Dialogue:

Audio:

Scene:

Shot: Duration:

Description/Dialogue:

Audio:

Scene:

Shot: Duration:

Description/Dialogue:

Audio:

Scene:

Shot: Duration:

Description/Dialogue:

Audio:

Scene:

Shot: Duration:

Description/Dialogue:

Audio:

Scene:

Shot: Duration:

Description/Dialogue:

Audio:

Scene:

Shot: Duration:

Description/Dialogue: _____

Audio: _____

Scene:

Shot: Duration:

Description/Dialogue: _____

Audio: _____

Scene:

Shot: Duration:

Description/Dialogue: _____

Audio: _____

Scene:

Shot: Duration:

Description/Dialogue: _____

Audio: _____

Scene:

Shot: Duration:

Description/Dialogue: _____

Audio: _____

Scene:

Shot: Duration:

Description/Dialogue: _____

Audio: _____

Scene:

Shot: Duration:

Description/Dialogue:

Audio:

Scene:

Shot: Duration:

Description/Dialogue:

Audio:

Scene:

Shot: Duration:

Description/Dialogue:

Audio:

Scene:

Shot: Duration:

Description/Dialogue:

Audio:

Scene:

Shot: Duration:

Description/Dialogue:

Audio:

Scene:

Shot: Duration:

Description/Dialogue:

Audio:

Scene:

Shot: Duration:

Description/Dialogue: _____

_____

Audio: _____

Scene:

Shot: Duration:

Description/Dialogue: _____

_____

Audio: _____

Scene:

Shot: Duration:

Description/Dialogue: _____

_____

Audio: _____

Scene:

Shot: Duration:

Description/Dialogue: _____

_____

Audio: _____

Scene:

Shot: Duration:

Description/Dialogue: _____

_____

Audio: _____

Scene:

Shot: Duration:

Description/Dialogue: _____

_____

Audio: _____

Scene:

Shot: Duration:

Description/Dialogue: _____

_____

Audio: _____

Scene:

Shot: Duration:

Description/Dialogue: _____

_____

Audio: _____

Scene:

Shot: Duration:

Description/Dialogue: _____

_____

Audio: _____

Scene:

Shot: Duration:

Description/Dialogue: _____

_____

Audio: _____

Scene:

Shot: Duration:

Description/Dialogue: _____

_____

Audio: _____

Scene:

Shot: Duration:

Description/Dialogue: _____

_____

Audio: _____

Scene:

Shot: Duration:

Description/Dialogue: _____

_____

Audio: _____

Scene:

Shot: Duration:

Description/Dialogue: _____

_____

Audio: _____

Scene:

Shot: Duration:

Description/Dialogue: _____

_____

Audio: _____

Scene:

Shot: Duration:

Description/Dialogue: _____

_____

Audio: _____

Scene:

Shot: Duration:

Description/Dialogue: _____

_____

Audio: _____

Scene:

Shot: Duration:

Description/Dialogue: _____

_____

Audio: _____

Scene:

Shot: Duration:

Description/Dialogue: _____

Audio: _____

Scene:

Shot: Duration:

Description/Dialogue: _____

Audio: _____

Scene:

Shot: Duration:

Description/Dialogue: _____

Audio: _____

Scene:

Shot: Duration:

Description/Dialogue: _____

Audio: _____

Scene:

Shot: Duration:

Description/Dialogue: _____

Audio: _____

Scene:

Shot: Duration:

Description/Dialogue: _____

Audio: _____

Scene:

Shot: Duration:

Description/Dialogue: —————————————

Audio: —————————————

Scene:

Shot: Duration:

Description/Dialogue: —————————————

Audio: —————————————

Scene:

Shot: Duration:

Description/Dialogue: —————————————

Audio: —————————————

Scene:

Shot: Duration:

Description/Dialogue: —————————————

Audio: —————————————

Scene:

Shot: Duration:

Description/Dialogue: —————————————

Audio: —————————————

Scene:

Shot: Duration:

Description/Dialogue: —————————————

Audio: —————————————

Scene:

Shot: Duration:

Description/Dialogue: _____

_____

Audio: _____

Scene:

Shot: Duration:

Description/Dialogue: _____

_____

Audio: _____

Scene:

Shot: Duration:

Description/Dialogue: _____

_____

Audio: _____

Scene:

Shot: Duration:

Description/Dialogue: _____

_____

Audio: _____

Scene:

Shot: Duration:

Description/Dialogue: _____

_____

Audio: _____

Scene:

Shot: Duration:

Description/Dialogue: _____

_____

Audio: _____

Scene:

Shot: | Duration:

Description/Dialogue: _____

Audio: _____

Scene:

Shot: | Duration:

Description/Dialogue: _____

Audio: _____

Scene:

Shot: | Duration:

Description/Dialogue: _____

Audio: _____

Scene:

Shot: | Duration:

Description/Dialogue: _____

Audio: _____

Scene:

Shot: | Duration:

Description/Dialogue: _____

Audio: _____

Scene:

Shot: | Duration:

Description/Dialogue: _____

Audio: _____

Scene:

Shot: Duration:

Description/Dialogue:

Audio:

Scene:

Shot: Duration:

Description/Dialogue:

Audio:

Scene:

Shot: Duration:

Description/Dialogue:

Audio:

Scene:

Shot: Duration:

Description/Dialogue:

Audio:

Scene:

Shot: Duration:

Description/Dialogue:

Audio:

Scene:

Shot: Duration:

Description/Dialogue:

Audio:

Scene:

Shot: Duration:

Description/Dialogue: —————————————

Audio: —————————————

Scene:

Shot: Duration:

Description/Dialogue: —————————————

Audio: —————————————

Scene:

Shot: Duration:

Description/Dialogue: —————————————

Audio: —————————————

Scene:

Shot: Duration:

Description/Dialogue: —————————————

Audio: —————————————

Scene:

Shot: Duration:

Description/Dialogue: —————————————

Audio: —————————————

Scene:

Shot: Duration:

Description/Dialogue: —————————————

Audio: —————————————

Scene:

Shot: Duration:

Description/Dialogue: _____

Audio: _____

Scene:

Shot: Duration:

Description/Dialogue: _____

Audio: _____

Scene:

Shot: Duration:

Description/Dialogue: _____

Audio: _____

Scene:

Shot: Duration:

Description/Dialogue: _____

Audio: _____

Scene:

Shot: Duration:

Description/Dialogue: _____

Audio: _____

Scene:

Shot: Duration:

Description/Dialogue: _____

Audio: _____

Scene:

Shot: Duration:

Description/Dialogue: _____

Audio: _____

Scene:

Shot: Duration:

Description/Dialogue: _____

Audio: _____

Scene:

Shot: Duration:

Description/Dialogue: _____

Audio: _____

Scene:

Shot: Duration:

Description/Dialogue: _____

Audio: _____

Scene:

Shot: Duration:

Description/Dialogue: _____

Audio: _____

Scene:

Shot: Duration:

Description/Dialogue: _____

Audio: _____

Scene:

Shot: Duration:

Description/Dialogue: _____

_____

_____

Audio: _____

Scene:

Shot: Duration:

Description/Dialogue: _____

_____

_____

Audio: _____

Scene:

Shot: Duration:

Description/Dialogue: _____

_____

_____

Audio: _____

Scene:

Shot: Duration:

Description/Dialogue: _____

_____

_____

Audio: _____

Scene:

Shot: Duration:

Description/Dialogue: _____

_____

_____

Audio: _____

Scene:

Shot: Duration:

Description/Dialogue: _____

_____

_____

Audio: _____

Scene:

Shot: Duration:

Description/Dialogue: _____

Audio: _____

Scene:

Shot: Duration:

Description/Dialogue: _____

Audio: _____

Scene:

Shot: Duration:

Description/Dialogue: _____

Audio: _____

Scene:

Shot: Duration:

Description/Dialogue: _____

Audio: _____

Scene:

Shot: Duration:

Description/Dialogue: _____

Audio: _____

Scene:

Shot: Duration:

Description/Dialogue: _____

Audio: _____

Scene:

Shot: Duration:

Description/Dialogue: _____

_____

Audio: _____

Scene:

Shot: Duration:

Description/Dialogue: _____

_____

Audio: _____

Scene:

Shot: Duration:

Description/Dialogue: _____

_____

Audio: _____

Scene:

Shot: Duration:

Description/Dialogue: _____

_____

Audio: _____

Scene:

Shot: Duration:

Description/Dialogue: _____

_____

Audio: _____

Scene:

Shot: Duration:

Description/Dialogue: _____

_____

Audio: _____

Scene:

Shot: Duration:

Description/Dialogue: ——————————————————————

—————————————————————————————————————

Audio: ————————————————————————————

Scene:

Shot: Duration:

Description/Dialogue: ——————————————————————

—————————————————————————————————————

Audio: ————————————————————————————

Scene:

Shot: Duration:

Description/Dialogue: ——————————————————————

—————————————————————————————————————

Audio: ————————————————————————————

Scene:

Shot: Duration:

Description/Dialogue: ——————————————————————

—————————————————————————————————————

Audio: ————————————————————————————

Scene:

Shot: Duration:

Description/Dialogue: ——————————————————————

—————————————————————————————————————

Audio: ————————————————————————————

Scene:

Shot: Duration:

Description/Dialogue: ——————————————————————

—————————————————————————————————————

Audio: ————————————————————————————

Scene:

Shot: Duration:

Description/Dialogue: _____

Audio: _____

Scene:

Shot: Duration:

Description/Dialogue: _____

Audio: _____

Scene:

Shot: Duration:

Description/Dialogue: _____

Audio: _____

Scene:

Shot: Duration:

Description/Dialogue: _____

Audio: _____

Scene:

Shot: Duration:

Description/Dialogue: _____

Audio: _____

Scene:

Shot: Duration:

Description/Dialogue: _____

Audio: _____

Scene:

Shot: Duration:

Description/Dialogue: —————————————

Audio: —————————————

Scene:

Shot: Duration:

Description/Dialogue: —————————————

Audio: —————————————

Scene:

Shot: Duration:

Description/Dialogue: —————————————

Audio: —————————————

Scene:

Shot: Duration:

Description/Dialogue: —————————————

Audio: —————————————

Scene:

Shot: Duration:

Description/Dialogue: —————————————

Audio: —————————————

Scene:

Shot: Duration:

Description/Dialogue: —————————————

Audio: —————————————

Scene:

Shot: Duration:

Description/Dialogue: _____

Audio: _____

Scene:

Shot: Duration:

Description/Dialogue: _____

Audio: _____

Scene:

Shot: Duration:

Description/Dialogue: _____

Audio: _____

Scene:

Shot: Duration:

Description/Dialogue: _____

Audio: _____

Scene:

Shot: Duration:

Description/Dialogue: _____

Audio: _____

Scene:

Shot: Duration:

Description/Dialogue: _____

Audio: _____

Scene:

Shot: | Duration:

Description/Dialogue: ————————

Audio: ———

Scene:

Shot: | Duration:

Description/Dialogue: ————————

Audio: ———

Scene:

Shot: | Duration:

Description/Dialogue: ————————

Audio: ———

Scene:

Shot: | Duration:

Description/Dialogue: ————————

Audio: ———

Scene:

Shot: | Duration:

Description/Dialogue: ————————

Audio: ———

Scene:

Shot: | Duration:

Description/Dialogue: ————————

Audio: ———

Scene:

Shot: Duration:

Description/Dialogue: _____

Audio: _____

Scene:

Shot: Duration:

Description/Dialogue: _____

Audio: _____

Scene:

Shot: Duration:

Description/Dialogue: _____

Audio: _____

Scene:

Shot: Duration:

Description/Dialogue: _____

Audio: _____

Scene:

Shot: Duration:

Description/Dialogue: _____

Audio: _____

Scene:

Shot: Duration:

Description/Dialogue: _____

Audio: _____

DATE:

Scene:

Shot: Duration:

Description/Dialogue: ⎯⎯⎯⎯⎯⎯⎯⎯⎯⎯

Audio: ⎯⎯⎯⎯⎯⎯⎯⎯⎯⎯

Scene:

Shot: Duration:

Description/Dialogue: ⎯⎯⎯⎯⎯⎯⎯⎯⎯⎯

Audio: ⎯⎯⎯⎯⎯⎯⎯⎯⎯⎯

Scene:

Shot: Duration:

Description/Dialogue: ⎯⎯⎯⎯⎯⎯⎯⎯⎯⎯

Audio: ⎯⎯⎯⎯⎯⎯⎯⎯⎯⎯

Scene:

Shot: Duration:

Description/Dialogue: ⎯⎯⎯⎯⎯⎯⎯⎯⎯⎯

Audio: ⎯⎯⎯⎯⎯⎯⎯⎯⎯⎯

Scene:

Shot: Duration:

Description/Dialogue: ⎯⎯⎯⎯⎯⎯⎯⎯⎯⎯

Audio: ⎯⎯⎯⎯⎯⎯⎯⎯⎯⎯

Scene:

Shot: Duration:

Description/Dialogue: ⎯⎯⎯⎯⎯⎯⎯⎯⎯⎯

Audio: ⎯⎯⎯⎯⎯⎯⎯⎯⎯⎯

Scene:

Shot: Duration:

Description/Dialogue: _____

_____

Audio: _____

Scene:

Shot: Duration:

Description/Dialogue: _____

_____

Audio: _____

Scene:

Shot: Duration:

Description/Dialogue: _____

_____

Audio: _____

Scene:

Shot: Duration:

Description/Dialogue: _____

_____

Audio: _____

Scene:

Shot: Duration:

Description/Dialogue: _____

_____

Audio: _____

Scene:

Shot: Duration:

Description/Dialogue: _____

_____

Audio: _____

Scene:

Shot: Duration:

Description/Dialogue: _____

Audio: _____

Scene:

Shot: Duration:

Description/Dialogue: _____

Audio: _____

Scene:

Shot: Duration:

Description/Dialogue: _____

Audio: _____

Scene:

Shot: Duration:

Description/Dialogue: _____

Audio: _____

Scene:

Shot: Duration:

Description/Dialogue: _____

Audio: _____

Scene:

Shot: Duration:

Description/Dialogue: _____

Audio: _____

Scene:

Shot: Duration:

Description/Dialogue: _____

_____

Audio: _____

Scene:

Shot: Duration:

Description/Dialogue: _____

_____

Audio: _____

Scene:

Shot: Duration:

Description/Dialogue: _____

_____

Audio: _____

Scene:

Shot: Duration:

Description/Dialogue: _____

_____

Audio: _____

Scene:

Shot: Duration:

Description/Dialogue: _____

_____

Audio: _____

Scene:

Shot: Duration:

Description/Dialogue: _____

_____

Audio: _____

Scene:

Shot: Duration:

Description/Dialogue: _____

Audio: _____

Scene:

Shot: Duration:

Description/Dialogue: _____

Audio: _____

Scene:

Shot: Duration:

Description/Dialogue: _____

Audio: _____

Scene:

Shot: Duration:

Description/Dialogue: _____

Audio: _____

Scene:

Shot: Duration:

Description/Dialogue: _____

Audio: _____

Scene:

Shot: Duration:

Description/Dialogue: _____

Audio: _____

Scene:

Shot: Duration:

Description/Dialogue: _____

Audio: _____

Scene:

Shot: Duration:

Description/Dialogue: _____

Audio: _____

Scene:

Shot: Duration:

Description/Dialogue: _____

Audio: _____

Scene:

Shot: Duration:

Description/Dialogue: _____

Audio: _____

Scene:

Shot: Duration:

Description/Dialogue: _____

Audio: _____

Scene:

Shot: Duration:

Description/Dialogue: _____

Audio: _____

Scene:

Shot: _____ Duration: _____

Description/Dialogue: _____

Audio: _____

Scene:

Shot: _____ Duration: _____

Description/Dialogue: _____

Audio: _____

Scene:

Shot: _____ Duration: _____

Description/Dialogue: _____

Audio: _____

Scene:

Shot: _____ Duration: _____

Description/Dialogue: _____

Audio: _____

Scene:

Shot: _____ Duration: _____

Description/Dialogue: _____

Audio: _____

Scene:

Shot: _____ Duration: _____

Description/Dialogue: _____

Audio: _____

Scene:

Shot: Duration:

Description/Dialogue: _____

Audio: _____

Scene:

Shot: Duration:

Description/Dialogue: _____

Audio: _____

Scene:

Shot: Duration:

Description/Dialogue: _____

Audio: _____

Scene:

Shot: Duration:

Description/Dialogue: _____

Audio: _____

Scene:

Shot: Duration:

Description/Dialogue: _____

Audio: _____

Scene:

Shot: Duration:

Description/Dialogue: _____

Audio: _____

Scene:

Shot: Duration:

Description/Dialogue: _____

_____

Audio: _____

Scene:

Shot: Duration:

Description/Dialogue: _____

_____

Audio: _____

Scene:

Shot: Duration:

Description/Dialogue: _____

_____

Audio: _____

Scene:

Shot: Duration:

Description/Dialogue: _____

_____

Audio: _____

Scene:

Shot: Duration:

Description/Dialogue: _____

_____

Audio: _____

Scene:

Shot: Duration:

Description/Dialogue: _____

_____

Audio: _____

Scene:

Shot: Duration:

Description/Dialogue: _____

Audio: _____

Scene:

Shot: Duration:

Description/Dialogue: _____

Audio: _____

Scene:

Shot: Duration:

Description/Dialogue: _____

Audio: _____

Scene:

Shot: Duration:

Description/Dialogue: _____

Audio: _____

Scene:

Shot: Duration:

Description/Dialogue: _____

Audio: _____

Scene:

Shot: Duration:

Description/Dialogue: _____

Audio: _____

Scene:

Shot: Duration:

Description/Dialogue:

Audio:

Scene:

Shot: Duration:

Description/Dialogue:

Audio:

Scene:

Shot: Duration:

Description/Dialogue:

Audio:

Scene:

Shot: Duration:

Description/Dialogue:

Audio:

Scene:

Shot: Duration:

Description/Dialogue:

Audio:

Scene:

Shot: Duration:

Description/Dialogue:

Audio:

Scene:

Shot: Duration:

Description/Dialogue:

Audio:

Scene:

Shot: Duration:

Description/Dialogue:

Audio:

Scene:

Shot: Duration:

Description/Dialogue:

Audio:

Scene:

Shot: Duration:

Description/Dialogue:

Audio:

Scene:

Shot: Duration:

Description/Dialogue:

Audio:

Scene:

Shot: Duration:

Description/Dialogue:

Audio:

Scene:

Shot: Duration:

Description/Dialogue: _____

_____

Audio: _____

Scene:

Shot: Duration:

Description/Dialogue: _____

_____

Audio: _____

Scene:

Shot: Duration:

Description/Dialogue: _____

_____

Audio: _____

Scene:

Shot: Duration:

Description/Dialogue: _____

_____

Audio: _____

Scene:

Shot: Duration:

Description/Dialogue: _____

_____

Audio: _____

Scene:

Shot: Duration:

Description/Dialogue: _____

_____

Audio: _____

Scene:

Shot: Duration:

Description/Dialogue: _____

Audio: _____

Scene:

Shot: Duration:

Description/Dialogue: _____

Audio: _____

Scene:

Shot: Duration:

Description/Dialogue: _____

Audio: _____

Scene:

Shot: Duration:

Description/Dialogue: _____

Audio: _____

Scene:

Shot: Duration:

Description/Dialogue: _____

Audio: _____

Scene:

Shot: Duration:

Description/Dialogue: _____

Audio: _____

Scene:

Shot: Duration:

Description/Dialogue: _____

Audio: _____

Scene:

Shot: Duration:

Description/Dialogue: _____

Audio: _____

Scene:

Shot: Duration:

Description/Dialogue: _____

Audio: _____

Scene:

Shot: Duration:

Description/Dialogue: _____

Audio: _____

Scene:

Shot: Duration:

Description/Dialogue: _____

Audio: _____

Scene:

Shot: Duration:

Description/Dialogue: _____

Audio: _____

| Scene: |
| Shot: | Duration: |

Description/Dialogue: _____

_____

Audio: _____

| Scene: |
| Shot: | Duration: |

Description/Dialogue: _____

_____

Audio: _____

| Scene: |
| Shot: | Duration: |

Description/Dialogue: _____

_____

Audio: _____

| Scene: |
| Shot: | Duration: |

Description/Dialogue: _____

_____

Audio: _____

| Scene: |
| Shot: | Duration: |

Description/Dialogue: _____

_____

Audio: _____

| Scene: |
| Shot: | Duration: |

Description/Dialogue: _____

_____

Audio: _____

Scene:

Shot: Duration:

Description/Dialogue: _____

Audio: _____

Scene:

Shot: Duration:

Description/Dialogue: _____

Audio: _____

Scene:

Shot: Duration:

Description/Dialogue: _____

Audio: _____

Scene:

Shot: Duration:

Description/Dialogue: _____

Audio: _____

Scene:

Shot: Duration:

Description/Dialogue: _____

Audio: _____

Scene:

Shot: Duration:

Description/Dialogue: _____

Audio: _____

Scene:

Shot: Duration:

Description/Dialogue: _____

Audio: _____

Scene:

Shot: Duration:

Description/Dialogue: _____

Audio: _____

Scene:

Shot: Duration:

Description/Dialogue: _____

Audio: _____

Scene:

Shot: Duration:

Description/Dialogue: _____

Audio: _____

Scene:

Shot: Duration:

Description/Dialogue: _____

Audio: _____

Scene:

Shot: Duration:

Description/Dialogue: _____

Audio: _____

Scene:

Shot: Duration:

Description/Dialogue: _____

Audio: _____

Scene:

Shot: Duration:

Description/Dialogue: _____

Audio: _____

Scene:

Shot: Duration:

Description/Dialogue: _____

Audio: _____

Scene:

Shot: Duration:

Description/Dialogue: _____

Audio: _____

Scene:

Shot: Duration:

Description/Dialogue: _____

Audio: _____

Scene:

Shot: Duration:

Description/Dialogue: _____

Audio: _____

Scene:

Shot: Duration:

Description/Dialogue: —————————————

Audio: —————————————

Scene:

Shot: Duration:

Description/Dialogue: —————————————

Audio: —————————————

Scene:

Shot: Duration:

Description/Dialogue: —————————————

Audio: —————————————

Scene:

Shot: Duration:

Description/Dialogue: —————————————

Audio: —————————————

Scene:

Shot: Duration:

Description/Dialogue: —————————————

Audio: —————————————

Scene:

Shot: Duration:

Description/Dialogue: —————————————

Audio: —————————————

Scene:

Shot: Duration:

Description/Dialogue:

Audio:

Scene:

Shot: Duration:

Description/Dialogue:

Audio:

Scene:

Shot: Duration:

Description/Dialogue:

Audio:

Scene:

Shot: Duration:

Description/Dialogue:

Audio:

Scene:

Shot: Duration:

Description/Dialogue:

Audio:

Scene:

Shot: Duration:

Description/Dialogue:

Audio:

Scene:

Shot: Duration:

Description/Dialogue: _____

_____

Audio: _____

Scene:

Shot: Duration:

Description/Dialogue: _____

_____

Audio: _____

Scene:

Shot: Duration:

Description/Dialogue: _____

_____

Audio: _____

Scene:

Shot: Duration:

Description/Dialogue: _____

_____

Audio: _____

Scene:

Shot: Duration:

Description/Dialogue: _____

_____

Audio: _____

Scene:

Shot: Duration:

Description/Dialogue: _____

_____

Audio: _____

Scene:

Shot: Duration:

Description/Dialogue: ——————————————

Audio: ————————————————————

Scene:

Shot: Duration:

Description/Dialogue: ——————————————

Audio: ————————————————————

Scene:

Shot: Duration:

Description/Dialogue: ——————————————

Audio: ————————————————————

Scene:

Shot: Duration:

Description/Dialogue: ——————————————

Audio: ————————————————————

Scene:

Shot: Duration:

Description/Dialogue: ——————————————

Audio: ————————————————————

Scene:

Shot: Duration:

Description/Dialogue: ——————————————

Audio: ————————————————————

Scene:

Shot: Duration:

Description/Dialogue:

Audio:

Scene:

Shot: Duration:

Description/Dialogue:

Audio:

Scene:

Shot: Duration:

Description/Dialogue:

Audio:

Scene:

Shot: Duration:

Description/Dialogue:

Audio:

Scene:

Shot: Duration:

Description/Dialogue:

Audio:

Scene:

Shot: Duration:

Description/Dialogue:

Audio:

Scene:

Shot: Duration:

Description/Dialogue: ————————————

Audio: ————————————————

Scene:

Shot: Duration:

Description/Dialogue: ————————————

Audio: ————————————————

Scene:

Shot: Duration:

Description/Dialogue: ————————————

Audio: ————————————————

Scene:

Shot: Duration:

Description/Dialogue: ————————————

Audio: ————————————————

Scene:

Shot: Duration:

Description/Dialogue: ————————————

Audio: ————————————————

Scene:

Shot: Duration:

Description/Dialogue: ————————————

Audio: ————————————————

Scene:

Shot: Duration:

Description/Dialogue: _____

_____

Audio: _____

Scene:

Shot: Duration:

Description/Dialogue: _____

_____

Audio: _____

Scene:

Shot: Duration:

Description/Dialogue: _____

_____

Audio: _____

Scene:

Shot: Duration:

Description/Dialogue: _____

_____

Audio: _____

Scene:

Shot: Duration:

Description/Dialogue: _____

_____

Audio: _____

Scene:

Shot: Duration:

Description/Dialogue: _____

_____

Audio: _____

Scene:

Shot: Duration:

Description/Dialogue: _____

Audio: _____

Scene:

Shot: Duration:

Description/Dialogue: _____

Audio: _____

Scene:

Shot: Duration:

Description/Dialogue: _____

Audio: _____

Scene:

Shot: Duration:

Description/Dialogue: _____

Audio: _____

Scene:

Shot: Duration:

Description/Dialogue: _____

Audio: _____

Scene:

Shot: Duration:

Description/Dialogue: _____

Audio: _____

Scene:

Shot: Duration:

Description/Dialogue: _____

Audio: _____

Scene:

Shot: Duration:

Description/Dialogue: _____

Audio: _____

Scene:

Shot: Duration:

Description/Dialogue: _____

Audio: _____

Scene:

Shot: Duration:

Description/Dialogue: _____

Audio: _____

Scene:

Shot: Duration:

Description/Dialogue: _____

Audio: _____

Scene:

Shot: Duration:

Description/Dialogue: _____

Audio: _____

Scene:

Shot: Duration:

Description/Dialogue: _____

_____

Audio: _____

Scene:

Shot: Duration:

Description/Dialogue: _____

_____

Audio: _____

Scene:

Shot: Duration:

Description/Dialogue: _____

_____

Audio: _____

Scene:

Shot: Duration:

Description/Dialogue: _____

_____

Audio: _____

Scene:

Shot: Duration:

Description/Dialogue: _____

_____

Audio: _____

Scene:

Shot: Duration:

Description/Dialogue: _____

_____

Audio: _____

Scene:

Shot: Duration:

Description/Dialogue: _____

Audio: _____

Scene:

Shot: Duration:

Description/Dialogue: _____

Audio: _____

Scene:

Shot: Duration:

Description/Dialogue: _____

Audio: _____

Scene:

Shot: Duration:

Description/Dialogue: _____

Audio: _____

Scene:

Shot: Duration:

Description/Dialogue: _____

Audio: _____

Scene:

Shot: Duration:

Description/Dialogue: _____

Audio: _____

Scene:

Shot: Duration:

Description/Dialogue: ————————

Audio: ————————

Scene:

Shot: Duration:

Description/Dialogue: ————————

Audio: ————————

Scene:

Shot: Duration:

Description/Dialogue: ————————

Audio: ————————

Scene:

Shot: Duration:

Description/Dialogue: ————————

Audio: ————————

Scene:

Shot: Duration:

Description/Dialogue: ————————

Audio: ————————

Scene:

Shot: Duration:

Description/Dialogue: ————————

Audio: ————————

Scene:

Shot: Duration:

Description/Dialogue: _____

_____

Audio: _____

Scene:

Shot: Duration:

Description/Dialogue: _____

_____

Audio: _____

Scene:

Shot: Duration:

Description/Dialogue: _____

_____

Audio: _____

Scene:

Shot: Duration:

Description/Dialogue: _____

_____

Audio: _____

Scene:

Shot: Duration:

Description/Dialogue: _____

_____

Audio: _____

Scene:

Shot: Duration:

Description/Dialogue: _____

_____

Audio: _____

Scene:

Shot: Duration:

Description/Dialogue: ————————————

Audio: ———————————————

Scene:

Shot: Duration:

Description/Dialogue: ————————————

Audio: ———————————————

Scene:

Shot: Duration:

Description/Dialogue: ————————————

Audio: ———————————————

Scene:

Shot: Duration:

Description/Dialogue: ————————————

Audio: ———————————————

Scene:

Shot: Duration:

Description/Dialogue: ————————————

Audio: ———————————————

Scene:

Shot: Duration:

Description/Dialogue: ————————————

Audio: ———————————————

Scene:

Shot: Duration:

Description/Dialogue: _____

_____

Audio: _____

Scene:

Shot: Duration:

Description/Dialogue: _____

_____

Audio: _____

Scene:

Shot: Duration:

Description/Dialogue: _____

_____

Audio: _____

Scene:

Shot: Duration:

Description/Dialogue: _____

_____

Audio: _____

Scene:

Shot: Duration:

Description/Dialogue: _____

_____

Audio: _____

Scene:

Shot: Duration:

Description/Dialogue: _____

_____

Audio: _____

Scene:

Shot:　　　　　　　　Duration:

Description/Dialogue: _____

Audio: _____

Scene:

Shot:　　　　　　　　Duration:

Description/Dialogue: _____

Audio: _____

Scene:

Shot:　　　　　　　　Duration:

Description/Dialogue: _____

Audio: _____

Scene:

Shot:　　　　　　　　Duration:

Description/Dialogue: _____

Audio: _____

Scene:

Shot:　　　　　　　　Duration:

Description/Dialogue: _____

Audio: _____

Scene:

Shot:　　　　　　　　Duration:

Description/Dialogue: _____

Audio: _____

Scene:

Shot: Duration:

Description/Dialogue: _____

Audio: _____

Scene:

Shot: Duration:

Description/Dialogue: _____

Audio: _____

Scene:

Shot: Duration:

Description/Dialogue: _____

Audio: _____

Scene:

Shot: Duration:

Description/Dialogue: _____

Audio: _____

Scene:

Shot: Duration:

Description/Dialogue: _____

Audio: _____

Scene:

Shot: Duration:

Description/Dialogue: _____

Audio: _____

Scene:

Shot: | Duration:

Description/Dialogue: ————————————

Audio: ————————————

Scene:

Shot: | Duration:

Description/Dialogue: ————————————

Audio: ————————————

Scene:

Shot: | Duration:

Description/Dialogue: ————————————

Audio: ————————————

Scene:

Shot: | Duration:

Description/Dialogue: ————————————

Audio: ————————————

Scene:

Shot: | Duration:

Description/Dialogue: ————————————

Audio: ————————————

Scene:

Shot: | Duration:

Description/Dialogue: ————————————

Audio: ————————————

Scene:

Shot: Duration:

Description/Dialogue: _____

Audio: _____

Scene:

Shot: Duration:

Description/Dialogue: _____

Audio: _____

Scene:

Shot: Duration:

Description/Dialogue: _____

Audio: _____

Scene:

Shot: Duration:

Description/Dialogue: _____

Audio: _____

Scene:

Shot: Duration:

Description/Dialogue: _____

Audio: _____

Scene:

Shot: Duration:

Description/Dialogue: _____

Audio: _____

Scene:

Shot: Duration:

Description/Dialogue: _____

_____

Audio: _____

Scene:

Shot: Duration:

Description/Dialogue: _____

_____

Audio: _____

Scene:

Shot: Duration:

Description/Dialogue: _____

_____

Audio: _____

Scene:

Shot: Duration:

Description/Dialogue: _____

_____

Audio: _____

Scene:

Shot: Duration:

Description/Dialogue: _____

_____

Audio: _____

Scene:

Shot: Duration:

Description/Dialogue: _____

_____

Audio: _____

Scene:

Shot: Duration:

Description/Dialogue:

Audio:

Scene:

Shot: Duration:

Description/Dialogue:

Audio:

Scene:

Shot: Duration:

Description/Dialogue:

Audio:

Scene:

Shot: Duration:

Description/Dialogue:

Audio:

Scene:

Shot: Duration:

Description/Dialogue:

Audio:

Scene:

Shot: Duration:

Description/Dialogue:

Audio:

Scene:

Shot: Duration:

Description/Dialogue: —————————————

Audio: —————————————————

Scene:

Shot: Duration:

Description/Dialogue: —————————————

Audio: —————————————————

Scene:

Shot: Duration:

Description/Dialogue: —————————————

Audio: —————————————————

Scene:

Shot: Duration:

Description/Dialogue: —————————————

Audio: —————————————————

Scene:

Shot: Duration:

Description/Dialogue: —————————————

Audio: —————————————————

Scene:

Shot: Duration:

Description/Dialogue: —————————————

Audio: —————————————————

TITLE: DATE: **113**

Scene:
Shot: Duration:

Description/Dialogue:

Audio:

Scene:
Shot: Duration:

Description/Dialogue:

Audio:

Scene:
Shot: Duration:

Description/Dialogue:

Audio:

Scene:
Shot: Duration:

Description/Dialogue:

Audio:

Scene:
Shot: Duration:

Description/Dialogue:

Audio:

Scene:
Shot: Duration:

Description/Dialogue:

Audio:

Scene:

Shot: Duration:

Description/Dialogue: —————————————

Audio: —————————————————

Scene:

Shot: Duration:

Description/Dialogue: —————————————

Audio: —————————————————

Scene:

Shot: Duration:

Description/Dialogue: —————————————

Audio: —————————————————

Scene:

Shot: Duration:

Description/Dialogue: —————————————

Audio: —————————————————

Scene:

Shot: Duration:

Description/Dialogue: —————————————

Audio: —————————————————

Scene:

Shot: Duration:

Description/Dialogue: —————————————

Audio: —————————————————

Scene:

Shot: Duration:

Description/Dialogue: _____

_____

Audio: _____

Scene:

Shot: Duration:

Description/Dialogue: _____

_____

Audio: _____

Scene:

Shot: Duration:

Description/Dialogue: _____

_____

Audio: _____

Scene:

Shot: Duration:

Description/Dialogue: _____

_____

Audio: _____

Scene:

Shot: Duration:

Description/Dialogue: _____

_____

Audio: _____

Scene:

Shot: Duration:

Description/Dialogue: _____

_____

Audio: _____

DATE:

Scene:

Shot: Duration:

Description/Dialogue:

Audio:

Scene:

Shot: Duration:

Description/Dialogue:

Audio:

Scene:

Shot: Duration:

Description/Dialogue:

Audio:

Scene:

Shot: Duration:

Description/Dialogue:

Audio:

Scene:

Shot: Duration:

Description/Dialogue:

Audio:

Scene:

Shot: Duration:

Description/Dialogue:

Audio:

Scene:

Shot: Duration:

Description/Dialogue:

Audio:

Scene:

Shot: Duration:

Description/Dialogue:

Audio:

Scene:

Shot: Duration:

Description/Dialogue:

Audio:

Scene:

Shot: Duration:

Description/Dialogue:

Audio:

Scene:

Shot: Duration:

Description/Dialogue:

Audio:

Scene:

Shot: Duration:

Description/Dialogue:

Audio:

Scene:

Shot: Duration:

Description/Dialogue: ——————————————————————

Audio: ———————————————————————————

Scene:

Shot: Duration:

Description/Dialogue: ——————————————————————

Audio: ———————————————————————————

Scene:

Shot: Duration:

Description/Dialogue: ——————————————————————

Audio: ———————————————————————————

Scene:

Shot: Duration:

Description/Dialogue: ——————————————————————

Audio: ———————————————————————————

Scene:

Shot: Duration:

Description/Dialogue: ——————————————————————

Audio: ———————————————————————————

Scene:

Shot: Duration:

Description/Dialogue: ——————————————————————

Audio: ———————————————————————————

Scene:

Shot: Duration:

Description/Dialogue:

Audio:

Scene:

Shot: Duration:

Description/Dialogue:

Audio:

Scene:

Shot: Duration:

Description/Dialogue:

Audio:

Scene:

Shot: Duration:

Description/Dialogue:

Audio:

Scene:

Shot: Duration:

Description/Dialogue:

Audio:

Scene:

Shot: Duration:

Description/Dialogue:

Audio:

Scene:

Shot: Duration:

Description/Dialogue: _____

_____

Audio: _____

Scene:

Shot: Duration:

Description/Dialogue: _____

_____

Audio: _____

Scene:

Shot: Duration:

Description/Dialogue: _____

_____

Audio: _____

Scene:

Shot: Duration:

Description/Dialogue: _____

_____

Audio: _____

Scene:

Shot: Duration:

Description/Dialogue: _____

_____

Audio: _____

Scene:

Shot: Duration:

Description/Dialogue: _____

_____

Audio: _____

Scene:

Shot: Duration:

Description/Dialogue: ————————————

Audio: ————————————

Scene:

Shot: Duration:

Description/Dialogue: ————————————

Audio: ————————————

Scene:

Shot: Duration:

Description/Dialogue: ————————————

Audio: ————————————

Scene:

Shot: Duration:

Description/Dialogue: ————————————

Audio: ————————————

Scene:

Shot: Duration:

Description/Dialogue: ————————————

Audio: ————————————

Scene:

Shot: Duration:

Description/Dialogue: ————————————

Audio: ————————————

Scene:

Shot: Duration:

Description/Dialogue: _____

Audio: _____

Scene:

Shot: Duration:

Description/Dialogue: _____

Audio: _____

Scene:

Shot: Duration:

Description/Dialogue: _____

Audio: _____

Scene:

Shot: Duration:

Description/Dialogue: _____

Audio: _____

Scene:

Shot: Duration:

Description/Dialogue: _____

Audio: _____

Scene:

Shot: Duration:

Description/Dialogue: _____

Audio: _____

Scene:

Shot: Duration:

Description/Dialogue: _____

Audio: _____

Scene:

Shot: Duration:

Description/Dialogue: _____

Audio: _____

Scene:

Shot: Duration:

Description/Dialogue: _____

Audio: _____

Scene:

Shot: Duration:

Description/Dialogue: _____

Audio: _____

Scene:

Shot: Duration:

Description/Dialogue: _____

Audio: _____

Scene:

Shot: Duration:

Description/Dialogue: _____

Audio: _____

Scene:

Shot: Duration:

Description/Dialogue:

Audio:

Scene:

Shot: Duration:

Description/Dialogue:

Audio:

Scene:

Shot: Duration:

Description/Dialogue:

Audio:

Scene:

Shot: Duration:

Description/Dialogue:

Audio:

Scene:

Shot: Duration:

Description/Dialogue:

Audio:

Scene:

Shot: Duration:

Description/Dialogue:

Audio:

Scene:

Shot: Duration:

Description/Dialogue:

Audio:

Scene:

Shot: Duration:

Description/Dialogue:

Audio:

Scene:

Shot: Duration:

Description/Dialogue:

Audio:

Scene:

Shot: Duration:

Description/Dialogue:

Audio:

Scene:

Shot: Duration:

Description/Dialogue:

Audio:

Scene:

Shot: Duration:

Description/Dialogue:

Audio:

Scene:

Shot: Duration:

Description/Dialogue: _____

_____

Audio: _____

Scene:

Shot: Duration:

Description/Dialogue: _____

_____

Audio: _____

Scene:

Shot: Duration:

Description/Dialogue: _____

_____

Audio: _____

Scene:

Shot: Duration:

Description/Dialogue: _____

_____

Audio: _____

Scene:

Shot: Duration:

Description/Dialogue: _____

_____

Audio: _____

Scene:

Shot: Duration:

Description/Dialogue: _____

_____

Audio: _____

Scene:

Shot: Duration:

Description/Dialogue: _____

_____

Audio: _____

Scene:

Shot: Duration:

Description/Dialogue: _____

_____

Audio: _____

Scene:

Shot: Duration:

Description/Dialogue: _____

_____

Audio: _____

Scene:

Shot: Duration:

Description/Dialogue: _____

_____

Audio: _____

Scene:

Shot: Duration:

Description/Dialogue: _____

_____

Audio: _____

Scene:

Shot: Duration:

Description/Dialogue: _____

_____

Audio: _____

Scene:

Shot: Duration:

Description/Dialogue: _____

_____

Audio: _____

Scene:

Shot: Duration:

Description/Dialogue: _____

_____

Audio: _____

Scene:

Shot: Duration:

Description/Dialogue: _____

_____

Audio: _____

Scene:

Shot: Duration:

Description/Dialogue: _____

_____

Audio: _____

Scene:

Shot: Duration:

Description/Dialogue: _____

_____

Audio: _____

Scene:

Shot: Duration:

Description/Dialogue: _____

_____

Audio: _____

Scene:

Shot: | Duration:

Description/Dialogue: _____

Audio: _____

Scene:

Shot: | Duration:

Description/Dialogue: _____

Audio: _____

Scene:

Shot: | Duration:

Description/Dialogue: _____

Audio: _____

Scene:

Shot: | Duration:

Description/Dialogue: _____

Audio: _____

Scene:

Shot: | Duration:

Description/Dialogue: _____

Audio: _____

Scene:

Shot: | Duration:

Description/Dialogue: _____

Audio: _____

Scene:

Shot: Duration:

Description/Dialogue: ————————————

Audio: ————————————————

Scene:

Shot: Duration:

Description/Dialogue: ————————————

Audio: ————————————————

Scene:

Shot: Duration:

Description/Dialogue: ————————————

Audio: ————————————————

Scene:

Shot: Duration:

Description/Dialogue: ————————————

Audio: ————————————————

Scene:

Shot: Duration:

Description/Dialogue: ————————————

Audio: ————————————————

Scene:

Shot: Duration:

Description/Dialogue: ————————————

Audio: ————————————————

Scene:

Shot: Duration:

Description/Dialogue:

Audio:

Scene:

Shot: Duration:

Description/Dialogue:

Audio:

Scene:

Shot: Duration:

Description/Dialogue:

Audio:

Scene:

Shot: Duration:

Description/Dialogue:

Audio:

Scene:

Shot: Duration:

Description/Dialogue:

Audio:

Scene:

Shot: Duration:

Description/Dialogue:

Audio:

Scene:

Shot: Duration:

Description/Dialogue: ——————————

Audio: ————————————————

Scene:

Shot: Duration:

Description/Dialogue: ——————————

Audio: ————————————————

Scene:

Shot: Duration:

Description/Dialogue: ——————————

Audio: ————————————————

Scene:

Shot: Duration:

Description/Dialogue: ——————————

Audio: ————————————————

Scene:

Shot: Duration:

Description/Dialogue: ——————————

Audio: ————————————————

Scene:

Shot: Duration:

Description/Dialogue: ——————————

Audio: ————————————————

Scene:

Shot: Duration:

Description/Dialogue: —————————————

——————————————

Audio: ———————————

Scene:

Shot: Duration:

Description/Dialogue: —————————————

——————————————

Audio: ———————————

Scene:

Shot: Duration:

Description/Dialogue: —————————————

——————————————

Audio: ———————————

Scene:

Shot: Duration:

Description/Dialogue: —————————————

——————————————

Audio: ———————————

Scene:

Shot: Duration:

Description/Dialogue: —————————————

——————————————

Audio: ———————————

Scene:

Shot: Duration:

Description/Dialogue: —————————————

——————————————

Audio: ———————————

Scene:

Shot: Duration:

Description/Dialogue: _____

Audio: _____

Scene:

Shot: Duration:

Description/Dialogue: _____

Audio: _____

Scene:

Shot: Duration:

Description/Dialogue: _____

Audio: _____

Scene:

Shot: Duration:

Description/Dialogue: _____

Audio: _____

Scene:

Shot: Duration:

Description/Dialogue: _____

Audio: _____

Scene:

Shot: Duration:

Description/Dialogue: _____

Audio: _____

Scene:

Shot: Duration:

Description/Dialogue: _____

_____

Audio: _____

Scene:

Shot: Duration:

Description/Dialogue: _____

_____

Audio: _____

Scene:

Shot: Duration:

Description/Dialogue: _____

_____

Audio: _____

Scene:

Shot: Duration:

Description/Dialogue: _____

_____

Audio: _____

Scene:

Shot: Duration:

Description/Dialogue: _____

_____

Audio: _____

Scene:

Shot: Duration:

Description/Dialogue: _____

_____

Audio: _____

Scene:

Shot: Duration:

Description/Dialogue: _____

Audio: _____

Scene:

Shot: Duration:

Description/Dialogue: _____

Audio: _____

Scene:

Shot: Duration:

Description/Dialogue: _____

Audio: _____

Scene:

Shot: Duration:

Description/Dialogue: _____

Audio: _____

Scene:

Shot: Duration:

Description/Dialogue: _____

Audio: _____

Scene:

Shot: Duration:

Description/Dialogue: _____

Audio: _____

Scene:

Shot: Duration:

Description/Dialogue: _____

_____

Audio: _____

Scene:

Shot: Duration:

Description/Dialogue: _____

_____

Audio: _____

Scene:

Shot: Duration:

Description/Dialogue: _____

_____

Audio: _____

Scene:

Shot: Duration:

Description/Dialogue: _____

_____

Audio: _____

Scene:

Shot: Duration:

Description/Dialogue: _____

_____

Audio: _____

Scene:

Shot: Duration:

Description/Dialogue: _____

_____

Audio: _____

Scene:

Shot: | Duration:

Description/Dialogue: _____

Audio: _____

Scene:

Shot: | Duration:

Description/Dialogue: _____

Audio: _____

Scene:

Shot: | Duration:

Description/Dialogue: _____

Audio: _____

Scene:

Shot: | Duration:

Description/Dialogue: _____

Audio: _____

Scene:

Shot: | Duration:

Description/Dialogue: _____

Audio: _____

Scene:

Shot: | Duration:

Description/Dialogue: _____

Audio: _____

Scene:

Shot: Duration:

Description/Dialogue: _____

_____

Audio: _____

Scene:

Shot: Duration:

Description/Dialogue: _____

_____

Audio: _____

Scene:

Shot: Duration:

Description/Dialogue: _____

_____

Audio: _____

Scene:

Shot: Duration:

Description/Dialogue: _____

_____

Audio: _____

Scene:

Shot: Duration:

Description/Dialogue: _____

_____

Audio: _____

Scene:

Shot: Duration:

Description/Dialogue: _____

_____

Audio: _____

Scene:

Shot: Duration:

Description/Dialogue: —————————————

Audio: ————————————————

Scene:

Shot: Duration:

Description/Dialogue: —————————————

Audio: ————————————————

Scene:

Shot: Duration:

Description/Dialogue: —————————————

Audio: ————————————————

Scene:

Shot: Duration:

Description/Dialogue: —————————————

Audio: ————————————————

Scene:

Shot: Duration:

Description/Dialogue: —————————————

Audio: ————————————————

Scene:

Shot: Duration:

Description/Dialogue: —————————————

Audio: ————————————————

Scene:

Shot: Duration:

Description/Dialogue:

Audio:

Scene:

Shot: Duration:

Description/Dialogue:

Audio:

Scene:

Shot: Duration:

Description/Dialogue:

Audio:

Scene:

Shot: Duration:

Description/Dialogue:

Audio:

Scene:

Shot: Duration:

Description/Dialogue:

Audio:

Scene:

Shot: Duration:

Description/Dialogue:

Audio:

Scene:

Shot: Duration:

Description/Dialogue: ———————————

Audio: ————————————————

Scene:

Shot: Duration:

Description/Dialogue: ———————————

Audio: ————————————————

Scene:

Shot: Duration:

Description/Dialogue: ———————————

Audio: ————————————————

Scene:

Shot: Duration:

Description/Dialogue: ———————————

Audio: ————————————————

Scene:

Shot: Duration:

Description/Dialogue: ———————————

Audio: ————————————————

Scene:

Shot: Duration:

Description/Dialogue: ———————————

Audio: ————————————————

Scene:

Shot: Duration:

Description/Dialogue: _____

_____

Audio: _____

Scene:

Shot: Duration:

Description/Dialogue: _____

_____

Audio: _____

Scene:

Shot: Duration:

Description/Dialogue: _____

_____

Audio: _____

Scene:

Shot: Duration:

Description/Dialogue: _____

_____

Audio: _____

Scene:

Shot: Duration:

Description/Dialogue: _____

_____

Audio: _____

Scene:

Shot: Duration:

Description/Dialogue: _____

_____

Audio: _____

Scene:

Shot: | Duration:

Description/Dialogue: _____

Audio: _____

Scene:

Shot: | Duration:

Description/Dialogue: _____

Audio: _____

Scene:

Shot: | Duration:

Description/Dialogue: _____

Audio: _____

Scene:

Shot: | Duration:

Description/Dialogue: _____

Audio: _____

Scene:

Shot: | Duration:

Description/Dialogue: _____

Audio: _____

Scene:

Shot: | Duration:

Description/Dialogue: _____

Audio: _____

Scene:

Shot: Duration:

Description/Dialogue: _____

_____

Audio: _____

Scene:

Shot: Duration:

Description/Dialogue: _____

_____

Audio: _____

Scene:

Shot: Duration:

Description/Dialogue: _____

_____

Audio: _____

Scene:

Shot: Duration:

Description/Dialogue: _____

_____

Audio: _____

Scene:

Shot: Duration:

Description/Dialogue: _____

_____

Audio: _____

Scene:

Shot: Duration:

Description/Dialogue: _____

_____

Audio: _____

Scene:

Shot: Duration:

Description/Dialogue: _____

_____

Audio: _____

Scene:

Shot: Duration:

Description/Dialogue: _____

_____

Audio: _____

Scene:

Shot: Duration:

Description/Dialogue: _____

_____

Audio: _____

Scene:

Shot: Duration:

Description/Dialogue: _____

_____

Audio: _____

Scene:

Shot: Duration:

Description/Dialogue: _____

_____

Audio: _____

Scene:

Shot: Duration:

Description/Dialogue: _____

_____

Audio: _____

Scene:

Shot: Duration:

Description/Dialogue: _____

_____

Audio: _____

Scene:

Shot: Duration:

Description/Dialogue: _____

_____

Audio: _____

Scene:

Shot: Duration:

Description/Dialogue: _____

_____

Audio: _____

Scene:

Shot: Duration:

Description/Dialogue: _____

_____

Audio: _____

Scene:

Shot: Duration:

Description/Dialogue: _____

_____

Audio: _____

Scene:

Shot: Duration:

Description/Dialogue: _____

_____

Audio: _____

Scene:

Shot: Duration:

Description/Dialogue: _____

_____

Audio: _____

Scene:

Shot: Duration:

Description/Dialogue: _____

_____

Audio: _____

Scene:

Shot: Duration:

Description/Dialogue: _____

_____

Audio: _____

Scene:

Shot: Duration:

Description/Dialogue: _____

_____

Audio: _____

Scene:

Shot: Duration:

Description/Dialogue: _____

_____

Audio: _____

Scene:

Shot: Duration:

Description/Dialogue: _____

_____

Audio: _____

TITLE: DATE:

Scene:

Shot: Duration:

Description/Dialogue:

Audio:

Scene:

Shot: Duration:

Description/Dialogue:

Audio:

Scene:

Shot: Duration:

Description/Dialogue:

Audio:

Scene:

Shot: Duration:

Description/Dialogue:

Audio:

Scene:

Shot: Duration:

Description/Dialogue:

Audio:

Scene:

Shot: Duration:

Description/Dialogue:

Audio:

Scene:

Shot: Duration:

Description/Dialogue: _____

_____

Audio: _____

Scene:

Shot: Duration:

Description/Dialogue: _____

_____

Audio: _____

Scene:

Shot: Duration:

Description/Dialogue: _____

_____

Audio: _____

Scene:

Shot: Duration:

Description/Dialogue: _____

_____

Audio: _____

Scene:

Shot: Duration:

Description/Dialogue: _____

_____

Audio: _____

Scene:

Shot: Duration:

Description/Dialogue: _____

_____

Audio: _____

Scene:

Shot: Duration:

Description/Dialogue: _____

_____

Audio: _____

Scene:

Shot: Duration:

Description/Dialogue: _____

_____

Audio: _____

Scene:

Shot: Duration:

Description/Dialogue: _____

_____

Audio: _____

Scene:

Shot: Duration:

Description/Dialogue: _____

_____

Audio: _____

Scene:

Shot: Duration:

Description/Dialogue: _____

_____

Audio: _____

Scene:

Shot: Duration:

Description/Dialogue: _____

_____

Audio: _____

Scene:

Shot: Duration:

Description/Dialogue: ————————————————————

Audio: ———————————————————————————

Scene:

Shot: Duration:

Description/Dialogue: ————————————————————

Audio: ———————————————————————————

Scene:

Shot: Duration:

Description/Dialogue: ————————————————————

Audio: ———————————————————————————

Scene:

Shot: Duration:

Description/Dialogue: ————————————————————

Audio: ———————————————————————————

Scene:

Shot: Duration:

Description/Dialogue: ————————————————————

Audio: ———————————————————————————

Scene:

Shot: Duration:

Description/Dialogue: ————————————————————

Audio: ———————————————————————————

Scene:

Shot: Duration:

Description/Dialogue: _____

_____

_____

Audio: _____

Scene:

Shot: Duration:

Description/Dialogue: _____

_____

_____

Audio: _____

Scene:

Shot: Duration:

Description/Dialogue: _____

_____

_____

Audio: _____

Scene:

Shot: Duration:

Description/Dialogue: _____

_____

_____

Audio: _____

Scene:

Shot: Duration:

Description/Dialogue: _____

_____

_____

Audio: _____

Scene:

Shot: Duration:

Description/Dialogue: _____

_____

_____

Audio: _____

Scene:

Shot: | Duration:

Description/Dialogue: _____

Audio: _____

Scene:

Shot: | Duration:

Description/Dialogue: _____

Audio: _____

Scene:

Shot: | Duration:

Description/Dialogue: _____

Audio: _____

Scene:

Shot: | Duration:

Description/Dialogue: _____

Audio: _____

Scene:

Shot: | Duration:

Description/Dialogue: _____

Audio: _____

Scene:

Shot: | Duration:

Description/Dialogue: _____

Audio: _____

Scene:

Shot: Duration:

Description/Dialogue:

Audio:

Scene:

Shot: Duration:

Description/Dialogue:

Audio:

Scene:

Shot: Duration:

Description/Dialogue:

Audio:

Scene:

Shot: Duration:

Description/Dialogue:

Audio:

Scene:

Shot: Duration:

Description/Dialogue:

Audio:

Scene:

Shot: Duration:

Description/Dialogue:

Audio:

Scene:

Shot: Duration:

Description/Dialogue: ―――――――――

Audio: ――――――――――――――

Scene:

Shot: Duration:

Description/Dialogue: ―――――――――

Audio: ――――――――――――――

Scene:

Shot: Duration:

Description/Dialogue: ―――――――――

Audio: ――――――――――――――

Scene:

Shot: Duration:

Description/Dialogue: ―――――――――

Audio: ――――――――――――――

Scene:

Shot: Duration:

Description/Dialogue: ―――――――――

Audio: ――――――――――――――

Scene:

Shot: Duration:

Description/Dialogue: ―――――――――

Audio: ――――――――――――――

Scene:

Shot: Duration:

Description/Dialogue: _____

_____

Audio: _____

Scene:

Shot: Duration:

Description/Dialogue: _____

_____

Audio: _____

Scene:

Shot: Duration:

Description/Dialogue: _____

_____

Audio: _____

Scene:

Shot: Duration:

Description/Dialogue: _____

_____

Audio: _____

Scene:

Shot: Duration:

Description/Dialogue: _____

_____

Audio: _____

Scene:

Shot: Duration:

Description/Dialogue: _____

_____

Audio: _____

Scene:

Shot: Duration:

Description/Dialogue:

Audio:

Scene:

Shot: Duration:

Description/Dialogue:

Audio:

Scene:

Shot: Duration:

Description/Dialogue:

Audio:

Scene:

Shot: Duration:

Description/Dialogue:

Audio:

Scene:

Shot: Duration:

Description/Dialogue:

Audio:

Scene:

Shot: Duration:

Description/Dialogue:

Audio:

Scene:

Shot: Duration:

Description/Dialogue: _____

Audio: _____

Scene:

Shot: Duration:

Description/Dialogue: _____

Audio: _____

Scene:

Shot: Duration:

Description/Dialogue: _____

Audio: _____

Scene:

Shot: Duration:

Description/Dialogue: _____

Audio: _____

Scene:

Shot: Duration:

Description/Dialogue: _____

Audio: _____

Scene:

Shot: Duration:

Description/Dialogue: _____

Audio: _____

Scene:

Shot: Duration:

Description/Dialogue: _____

Audio: _____

Scene:

Shot: Duration:

Description/Dialogue: _____

Audio: _____

Scene:

Shot: Duration:

Description/Dialogue: _____

Audio: _____

Scene:

Shot: Duration:

Description/Dialogue: _____

Audio: _____

Scene:

Shot: Duration:

Description/Dialogue: _____

Audio: _____

Scene:

Shot: Duration:

Description/Dialogue: _____

Audio: _____

Scene:

Shot: Duration:

Description/Dialogue:

Audio:

Scene:

Shot: Duration:

Description/Dialogue:

Audio:

Scene:

Shot: Duration:

Description/Dialogue:

Audio:

Scene:

Shot: Duration:

Description/Dialogue:

Audio:

Scene:

Shot: Duration:

Description/Dialogue:

Audio:

Scene:

Shot: Duration:

Description/Dialogue:

Audio:

Scene:

Shot: Duration:

Description/Dialogue: _____

_____

Audio: _____

Scene:

Shot: Duration:

Description/Dialogue: _____

_____

Audio: _____

Scene:

Shot: Duration:

Description/Dialogue: _____

_____

Audio: _____

Scene:

Shot: Duration:

Description/Dialogue: _____

_____

Audio: _____

Scene:

Shot: Duration:

Description/Dialogue: _____

_____

Audio: _____

Scene:

Shot: Duration:

Description/Dialogue: _____

_____

Audio: _____

Scene:

Shot: Duration:

Description/Dialogue: _____

_____

Audio: _____

Scene:

Shot: Duration:

Description/Dialogue: _____

_____

Audio: _____

Scene:

Shot: Duration:

Description/Dialogue: _____

_____

Audio: _____

Scene:

Shot: Duration:

Description/Dialogue: _____

_____

Audio: _____

Scene:

Shot: Duration:

Description/Dialogue: _____

_____

Audio: _____

Scene:

Shot: Duration:

Description/Dialogue: _____

_____

Audio: _____

Scene:

Shot: Duration:

Description/Dialogue:

Audio:

Scene:

Shot: Duration:

Description/Dialogue:

Audio:

Scene:

Shot: Duration:

Description/Dialogue:

Audio:

Scene:

Shot: Duration:

Description/Dialogue:

Audio:

Scene:

Shot: Duration:

Description/Dialogue:

Audio:

Scene:

Shot: Duration:

Description/Dialogue:

Audio:

Scene:

Shot: | Duration:

Description/Dialogue: _____

_____

Audio: _____

Scene:

Shot: | Duration:

Description/Dialogue: _____

_____

Audio: _____

Scene:

Shot: | Duration:

Description/Dialogue: _____

_____

Audio: _____

Scene:

Shot: | Duration:

Description/Dialogue: _____

_____

Audio: _____

Scene:

Shot: | Duration:

Description/Dialogue: _____

_____

Audio: _____

Scene:

Shot: | Duration:

Description/Dialogue: _____

_____

Audio: _____

Scene:

Shot: Duration:

Description/Dialogue:

Audio:

Scene:

Shot: Duration:

Description/Dialogue:

Audio:

Scene:

Shot: Duration:

Description/Dialogue:

Audio:

Scene:

Shot: Duration:

Description/Dialogue:

Audio:

Scene:

Shot: Duration:

Description/Dialogue:

Audio:

Scene:

Shot: Duration:

Description/Dialogue:

Audio:

Scene:

Shot: Duration:

Description/Dialogue:

Audio:

Scene:

Shot: Duration:

Description/Dialogue:

Audio:

Scene:

Shot: Duration:

Description/Dialogue:

Audio:

Scene:

Shot: Duration:

Description/Dialogue:

Audio:

Scene:

Shot: Duration:

Description/Dialogue:

Audio:

Scene:

Shot: Duration:

Description/Dialogue:

Audio:

Scene:

Shot: Duration:

Description/Dialogue: _____

Audio: _____

Scene:

Shot: Duration:

Description/Dialogue: _____

Audio: _____

Scene:

Shot: Duration:

Description/Dialogue: _____

Audio: _____

Scene:

Shot: Duration:

Description/Dialogue: _____

Audio: _____

Scene:

Shot: Duration:

Description/Dialogue: _____

Audio: _____

Scene:

Shot: Duration:

Description/Dialogue: _____

Audio: _____

Scene:

Shot: Duration:

Description/Dialogue: _____

_____

Audio: _____

Scene:

Shot: Duration:

Description/Dialogue: _____

_____

Audio: _____

Scene:

Shot: Duration:

Description/Dialogue: _____

_____

Audio: _____

Scene:

Shot: Duration:

Description/Dialogue: _____

_____

Audio: _____

Scene:

Shot: Duration:

Description/Dialogue: _____

_____

Audio: _____

Scene:

Shot: Duration:

Description/Dialogue: _____

_____

Audio: _____

Scene:

Shot: Duration:

Description/Dialogue: _____

Audio: _____

Scene:

Shot: Duration:

Description/Dialogue: _____

Audio: _____

Scene:

Shot: Duration:

Description/Dialogue: _____

Audio: _____

Scene:

Shot: Duration:

Description/Dialogue: _____

Audio: _____

Scene:

Shot: Duration:

Description/Dialogue: _____

Audio: _____

Scene:

Shot: Duration:

Description/Dialogue: _____

Audio: _____

Scene:

Shot: Duration:

Description/Dialogue:

Audio:

Scene:

Shot: Duration:

Description/Dialogue:

Audio:

Scene:

Shot: Duration:

Description/Dialogue:

Audio:

Scene:

Shot: Duration:

Description/Dialogue:

Audio:

Scene:

Shot: Duration:

Description/Dialogue:

Audio:

Scene:

Shot: Duration:

Description/Dialogue:

Audio:

Scene:

Shot: Duration:

Description/Dialogue:

Audio:

Scene:

Shot: Duration:

Description/Dialogue:

Audio:

Scene:

Shot: Duration:

Description/Dialogue:

Audio:

Scene:

Shot: Duration:

Description/Dialogue:

Audio:

Scene:

Shot: Duration:

Description/Dialogue:

Audio:

Scene:

Shot: Duration:

Description/Dialogue:

Audio:

Scene:

Shot: Duration:

Description/Dialogue: _____

Audio: _____

Scene:

Shot: Duration:

Description/Dialogue: _____

Audio: _____

Scene:

Shot: Duration:

Description/Dialogue: _____

Audio: _____

Scene:

Shot: Duration:

Description/Dialogue: _____

Audio: _____

Scene:

Shot: Duration:

Description/Dialogue: _____

Audio: _____

Scene:

Shot: Duration:

Description/Dialogue: _____

Audio: _____

Scene:

Shot: Duration:

Description/Dialogue: _____

_____

Audio: _____

Scene:

Shot: Duration:

Description/Dialogue: _____

_____

Audio: _____

Scene:

Shot: Duration:

Description/Dialogue: _____

_____

Audio: _____

Scene:

Shot: Duration:

Description/Dialogue: _____

_____

Audio: _____

Scene:

Shot: Duration:

Description/Dialogue: _____

_____

Audio: _____

Scene:

Shot: Duration:

Description/Dialogue: _____

_____

Audio: _____

Scene:

Shot: Duration:

Description/Dialogue:

Audio:

Scene:

Shot: Duration:

Description/Dialogue:

Audio:

Scene:

Shot: Duration:

Description/Dialogue:

Audio:

Scene:

Shot: Duration:

Description/Dialogue:

Audio:

Scene:

Shot: Duration:

Description/Dialogue:

Audio:

Scene:

Shot: Duration:

Description/Dialogue:

Audio:

Scene:

Shot: Duration:

Description/Dialogue: ——————————————

Audio: ————————————————

Scene:

Shot: Duration:

Description/Dialogue: ——————————————

Audio: ————————————————

Scene:

Shot: Duration:

Description/Dialogue: ——————————————

Audio: ————————————————

Scene:

Shot: Duration:

Description/Dialogue: ——————————————

Audio: ————————————————

Scene:

Shot: Duration:

Description/Dialogue: ——————————————

Audio: ————————————————

Scene:

Shot: Duration:

Description/Dialogue: ——————————————

Audio: ————————————————

Scene:

Shot: Duration:

Description/Dialogue: _____

_____

Audio: _____

Scene:

Shot: Duration:

Description/Dialogue: _____

_____

Audio: _____

Scene:

Shot: Duration:

Description/Dialogue: _____

_____

Audio: _____

Scene:

Shot: Duration:

Description/Dialogue: _____

_____

Audio: _____

Scene:

Shot: Duration:

Description/Dialogue: _____

_____

Audio: _____

Scene:

Shot: Duration:

Description/Dialogue: _____

_____

Audio: _____

Scene:

Shot: Duration:

Description/Dialogue: ⸻

Audio: ⸻

Scene:

Shot: Duration:

Description/Dialogue: ⸻

Audio: ⸻

Scene:

Shot: Duration:

Description/Dialogue: ⸻

Audio: ⸻

Scene:

Shot: Duration:

Description/Dialogue: ⸻

Audio: ⸻

Scene:

Shot: Duration:

Description/Dialogue: ⸻

Audio: ⸻

Scene:

Shot: Duration:

Description/Dialogue: ⸻

Audio: ⸻

Scene:

Shot: Duration:

Description/Dialogue:

Audio:

Scene:

Shot: Duration:

Description/Dialogue:

Audio:

Scene:

Shot: Duration:

Description/Dialogue:

Audio:

Scene:

Shot: Duration:

Description/Dialogue:

Audio:

Scene:

Shot: Duration:

Description/Dialogue:

Audio:

Scene:

Shot: Duration:

Description/Dialogue:

Audio:

Scene:

Shot: Duration:

Description/Dialogue:

Audio:

Scene:

Shot: Duration:

Description/Dialogue:

Audio:

Scene:

Shot: Duration:

Description/Dialogue:

Audio:

Scene:

Shot: Duration:

Description/Dialogue:

Audio:

Scene:

Shot: Duration:

Description/Dialogue:

Audio:

Scene:

Shot: Duration:

Description/Dialogue:

Audio:

Scene:

Shot: Duration:

Description/Dialogue:

Audio:

Scene:

Shot: Duration:

Description/Dialogue:

Audio:

Scene:

Shot: Duration:

Description/Dialogue:

Audio:

Scene:

Shot: Duration:

Description/Dialogue:

Audio:

Scene:

Shot: Duration:

Description/Dialogue:

Audio:

Scene:

Shot: Duration:

Description/Dialogue:

Audio:

Scene:

Shot: Duration:

Description/Dialogue:

Audio:

Scene:

Shot: Duration:

Description/Dialogue:

Audio:

Scene:

Shot: Duration:

Description/Dialogue:

Audio:

Scene:

Shot: Duration:

Description/Dialogue:

Audio:

Scene:

Shot: Duration:

Description/Dialogue:

Audio:

Scene:

Shot: Duration:

Description/Dialogue:

Audio:

Scene:

Shot: Duration:

Description/Dialogue: _____

_____

Audio: _____

Scene:

Shot: Duration:

Description/Dialogue: _____

_____

Audio: _____

Scene:

Shot: Duration:

Description/Dialogue: _____

_____

Audio: _____

Scene:

Shot: Duration:

Description/Dialogue: _____

_____

Audio: _____

Scene:

Shot: Duration:

Description/Dialogue: _____

_____

Audio: _____

Scene:

Shot: Duration:

Description/Dialogue: _____

_____

Audio: _____

Scene:

Shot: | Duration:

Description/Dialogue: _____

Audio: _____

Scene:

Shot: | Duration:

Description/Dialogue: _____

Audio: _____

Scene:

Shot: | Duration:

Description/Dialogue: _____

Audio: _____

Scene:

Shot: | Duration:

Description/Dialogue: _____

Audio: _____

Scene:

Shot: | Duration:

Description/Dialogue: _____

Audio: _____

Scene:

Shot: | Duration:

Description/Dialogue: _____

Audio: _____

Scene:

Shot: Duration:

Description/Dialogue: _____

Audio: _____

Scene:

Shot: Duration:

Description/Dialogue: _____

Audio: _____

Scene:

Shot: Duration:

Description/Dialogue: _____

Audio: _____

Scene:

Shot: Duration:

Description/Dialogue: _____

Audio: _____

Scene:

Shot: Duration:

Description/Dialogue: _____

Audio: _____

Scene:

Shot: Duration:

Description/Dialogue: _____

Audio: _____

Scene:

Shot: Duration:

Description/Dialogue: _____

Audio: _____

Scene:

Shot: Duration:

Description/Dialogue: _____

Audio: _____

Scene:

Shot: Duration:

Description/Dialogue: _____

Audio: _____

Scene:

Shot: Duration:

Description/Dialogue: _____

Audio: _____

Scene:

Shot: Duration:

Description/Dialogue: _____

Audio: _____

Scene:

Shot: Duration:

Description/Dialogue: _____

Audio: _____

Scene:

Shot: Duration:

Description/Dialogue:

Audio:

Scene:

Shot: Duration:

Description/Dialogue:

Audio:

Scene:

Shot: Duration:

Description/Dialogue:

Audio:

Scene:

Shot: Duration:

Description/Dialogue:

Audio:

Scene:

Shot: Duration:

Description/Dialogue:

Audio:

Scene:

Shot: Duration:

Description/Dialogue:

Audio:

Scene:

Shot: | Duration:

Description/Dialogue: _____

Audio: _____

Scene:

Shot: | Duration:

Description/Dialogue: _____

Audio: _____

Scene:

Shot: | Duration:

Description/Dialogue: _____

Audio: _____

Scene:

Shot: | Duration:

Description/Dialogue: _____

Audio: _____

Scene:

Shot: | Duration:

Description/Dialogue: _____

Audio: _____

Scene:

Shot: | Duration:

Description/Dialogue: _____

Audio: _____

TITLE: _____ DATE: _____ **189**

Scene:
Shot: _____ | Duration: _____

Description/Dialogue: _____

Audio: _____

Scene:
Shot: _____ | Duration: _____

Description/Dialogue: _____

Audio: _____

Scene:
Shot: _____ | Duration: _____

Description/Dialogue: _____

Audio: _____

Scene:
Shot: _____ | Duration: _____

Description/Dialogue: _____

Audio: _____

Scene:
Shot: _____ | Duration: _____

Description/Dialogue: _____

Audio: _____

Scene:
Shot: _____ | Duration: _____

Description/Dialogue: _____

Audio: _____

Scene:

Shot: Duration:

Description/Dialogue: ——————————————

——————————————————————————————

Audio: ——————————————————————

Scene:

Shot: Duration:

Description/Dialogue: ——————————————

——————————————————————————————

Audio: ——————————————————————

Scene:

Shot: Duration:

Description/Dialogue: ——————————————

——————————————————————————————

Audio: ——————————————————————

Scene:

Shot: Duration:

Description/Dialogue: ——————————————

——————————————————————————————

Audio: ——————————————————————

Scene:

Shot: Duration:

Description/Dialogue: ——————————————

——————————————————————————————

Audio: ——————————————————————

Scene:

Shot: Duration:

Description/Dialogue: ——————————————

——————————————————————————————

Audio: ——————————————————————

Scene:

Shot: Duration:

Description/Dialogue: _____

_____

Audio: _____

Scene:

Shot: Duration:

Description/Dialogue: _____

_____

Audio: _____

Scene:

Shot: Duration:

Description/Dialogue: _____

_____

Audio: _____

Scene:

Shot: Duration:

Description/Dialogue: _____

_____

Audio: _____

Scene:

Shot: Duration:

Description/Dialogue: _____

_____

Audio: _____

Scene:

Shot: Duration:

Description/Dialogue: _____

_____

Audio: _____

Scene:

Shot: | Duration:

Description/Dialogue: _____

Audio: _____

Scene:

Shot: | Duration:

Description/Dialogue: _____

Audio: _____

Scene:

Shot: | Duration:

Description/Dialogue: _____

Audio: _____

Scene:

Shot: | Duration:

Description/Dialogue: _____

Audio: _____

Scene:

Shot: | Duration:

Description/Dialogue: _____

Audio: _____

Scene:

Shot: | Duration:

Description/Dialogue: _____

Audio: _____

Scene:

Shot: Duration:

Description/Dialogue: _____

Audio: _____

Scene:

Shot: Duration:

Description/Dialogue: _____

Audio: _____

Scene:

Shot: Duration:

Description/Dialogue: _____

Audio: _____

Scene:

Shot: Duration:

Description/Dialogue: _____

Audio: _____

Scene:

Shot: Duration:

Description/Dialogue: _____

Audio: _____

Scene:

Shot: Duration:

Description/Dialogue: _____

Audio: _____

Scene:

Shot: Duration:

Description/Dialogue: _____

_____

Audio: _____

Scene:

Shot: Duration:

Description/Dialogue: _____

_____

Audio: _____

Scene:

Shot: Duration:

Description/Dialogue: _____

_____

Audio: _____

Scene:

Shot: Duration:

Description/Dialogue: _____

_____

Audio: _____

Scene:

Shot: Duration:

Description/Dialogue: _____

_____

Audio: _____

Scene:

Shot: Duration:

Description/Dialogue: _____

_____

Audio: _____

Scene:

Shot: Duration:

Description/Dialogue:

Audio:

Scene:

Shot: Duration:

Description/Dialogue:

Audio:

Scene:

Shot: Duration:

Description/Dialogue:

Audio:

Scene:

Shot: Duration:

Description/Dialogue:

Audio:

Scene:

Shot: Duration:

Description/Dialogue:

Audio:

Scene:

Shot: Duration:

Description/Dialogue:

Audio:

Scene:

Shot: Duration:

Description/Dialogue: _____

Audio: _____

Scene:

Shot: Duration:

Description/Dialogue: _____

Audio: _____

Scene:

Shot: Duration:

Description/Dialogue: _____

Audio: _____

Scene:

Shot: Duration:

Description/Dialogue: _____

Audio: _____

Scene:

Shot: Duration:

Description/Dialogue: _____

Audio: _____

Scene:

Shot: Duration:

Description/Dialogue: _____

Audio: _____

Scene:

Shot: | Duration:

Description/Dialogue: _____

_____

Audio: _____

Scene:

Shot: | Duration:

Description/Dialogue: _____

_____

Audio: _____

Scene:

Shot: | Duration:

Description/Dialogue: _____

_____

Audio: _____

Scene:

Shot: | Duration:

Description/Dialogue: _____

_____

Audio: _____

Scene:

Shot: | Duration:

Description/Dialogue: _____

_____

Audio: _____

Scene:

Shot: | Duration:

Description/Dialogue: _____

_____

Audio: _____

Scene:

Shot: Duration:

Description/Dialogue: _____

Audio: _____

Scene:

Shot: Duration:

Description/Dialogue: _____

Audio: _____

Scene:

Shot: Duration:

Description/Dialogue: _____

Audio: _____

Scene:

Shot: Duration:

Description/Dialogue: _____

Audio: _____

Scene:

Shot: Duration:

Description/Dialogue: _____

Audio: _____

Scene:

Shot: Duration:

Description/Dialogue: _____

Audio: _____

Scene:

Shot: Duration:

Description/Dialogue: —————————————

Audio: —————————————

Scene:

Shot: Duration:

Description/Dialogue: —————————————

Audio: —————————————

Scene:

Shot: Duration:

Description/Dialogue: —————————————

Audio: —————————————

Scene:

Shot: Duration:

Description/Dialogue: —————————————

Audio: —————————————

Scene:

Shot: Duration:

Description/Dialogue: —————————————

Audio: —————————————

Scene:

Shot: Duration:

Description/Dialogue: —————————————

Audio: —————————————

Scene:

Shot: Duration:

Description/Dialogue: _____

Audio: _____

Scene:

Shot: Duration:

Description/Dialogue: _____

Audio: _____

Scene:

Shot: Duration:

Description/Dialogue: _____

Audio: _____

Scene:

Shot: Duration:

Description/Dialogue: _____

Audio: _____

Scene:

Shot: Duration:

Description/Dialogue: _____

Audio: _____

Scene:

Shot: Duration:

Description/Dialogue: _____

Audio: _____

Scene:

Shot: Duration:

Description/Dialogue: _____

_____

Audio: _____

Scene:

Shot: Duration:

Description/Dialogue: _____

_____

Audio: _____

Scene:

Shot: Duration:

Description/Dialogue: _____

_____

Audio: _____

Scene:

Shot: Duration:

Description/Dialogue: _____

_____

Audio: _____

Scene:

Shot: Duration:

Description/Dialogue: _____

_____

Audio: _____

Scene:

Shot: Duration:

Description/Dialogue: _____

_____

Audio: _____

Scene:

Shot: Duration:

Description/Dialogue:

Audio:

Scene:

Shot: Duration:

Description/Dialogue:

Audio:

Scene:

Shot: Duration:

Description/Dialogue:

Audio:

Scene:

Shot: Duration:

Description/Dialogue:

Audio:

Scene:

Shot: Duration:

Description/Dialogue:

Audio:

Scene:

Shot: Duration:

Description/Dialogue:

Audio:

Scene:

Shot: Duration:

Description/Dialogue:

Audio:

Scene:

Shot: Duration:

Description/Dialogue:

Audio:

Scene:

Shot: Duration:

Description/Dialogue:

Audio:

Scene:

Shot: Duration:

Description/Dialogue:

Audio:

Scene:

Shot: Duration:

Description/Dialogue:

Audio:

Scene:

Shot: Duration:

Description/Dialogue:

Audio:

Scene:

Shot: Duration:

Description/Dialogue: _____

Audio: _____

Scene:

Shot: Duration:

Description/Dialogue: _____

Audio: _____

Scene:

Shot: Duration:

Description/Dialogue: _____

Audio: _____

Scene:

Shot: Duration:

Description/Dialogue: _____

Audio: _____

Scene:

Shot: Duration:

Description/Dialogue: _____

Audio: _____

Scene:

Shot: Duration:

Description/Dialogue: _____

Audio: _____

Scene:

Shot: | Duration:

Description/Dialogue: _____

Audio: _____

Scene:

Shot: | Duration:

Description/Dialogue: _____

Audio: _____

Scene:

Shot: | Duration:

Description/Dialogue: _____

Audio: _____

Scene:

Shot: | Duration:

Description/Dialogue: _____

Audio: _____

Scene:

Shot: | Duration:

Description/Dialogue: _____

Audio: _____

Scene:

Shot: | Duration:

Description/Dialogue: _____

Audio: _____

Scene:

Shot: Duration:

Description/Dialogue: _____

_____

Audio: _____

Scene:

Shot: Duration:

Description/Dialogue: _____

_____

Audio: _____

Scene:

Shot: Duration:

Description/Dialogue: _____

_____

Audio: _____

Scene:

Shot: Duration:

Description/Dialogue: _____

_____

Audio: _____

Scene:

Shot: Duration:

Description/Dialogue: _____

_____

Audio: _____

Scene:

Shot: Duration:

Description/Dialogue: _____

_____

Audio: _____

Scene:

Shot: Duration:

Description/Dialogue:

Audio:

Scene:

Shot: Duration:

Description/Dialogue:

Audio:

Scene:

Shot: Duration:

Description/Dialogue:

Audio:

Scene:

Shot: Duration:

Description/Dialogue:

Audio:

Scene:

Shot: Duration:

Description/Dialogue:

Audio:

Scene:

Shot: Duration:

Description/Dialogue:

Audio:

DATE:

Scene:

Shot: Duration:

Description/Dialogue: _____

Audio: _____

Scene:

Shot: Duration:

Description/Dialogue: _____

Audio: _____

Scene:

Shot: Duration:

Description/Dialogue: _____

Audio: _____

Scene:

Shot: Duration:

Description/Dialogue: _____

Audio: _____

Scene:

Shot: Duration:

Description/Dialogue: _____

Audio: _____

Scene:

Shot: Duration:

Description/Dialogue: _____

Audio: _____

Scene:

Shot: Duration:

Description/Dialogue: _____

_____

Audio: _____

Scene:

Shot: Duration:

Description/Dialogue: _____

_____

Audio: _____

Scene:

Shot: Duration:

Description/Dialogue: _____

_____

Audio: _____

Scene:

Shot: Duration:

Description/Dialogue: _____

_____

Audio: _____

Scene:

Shot: Duration:

Description/Dialogue: _____

_____

Audio: _____

Scene:

Shot: Duration:

Description/Dialogue: _____

_____

Audio: _____

Scene:

Shot: Duration:

Description/Dialogue: _____

Audio: _____

Scene:

Shot: Duration:

Description/Dialogue: _____

Audio: _____

Scene:

Shot: Duration:

Description/Dialogue: _____

Audio: _____

Scene:

Shot: Duration:

Description/Dialogue: _____

Audio: _____

Scene:

Shot: Duration:

Description/Dialogue: _____

Audio: _____

Scene:

Shot: Duration:

Description/Dialogue: _____

Audio: _____

TITLE: _____ DATE: _____

Scene:
Shot: _____ Duration: _____

Description/Dialogue: _____

Audio: _____

Scene:
Shot: _____ Duration: _____

Description/Dialogue: _____

Audio: _____

Scene:
Shot: _____ Duration: _____

Description/Dialogue: _____

Audio: _____

Scene:
Shot: _____ Duration: _____

Description/Dialogue: _____

Audio: _____

Scene:
Shot: _____ Duration: _____

Description/Dialogue: _____

Audio: _____

Scene:
Shot: _____ Duration: _____

Description/Dialogue: _____

Audio: _____

Scene:

Shot: Duration:

Description/Dialogue: —————————————

Audio: ———————

Scene:

Shot: Duration:

Description/Dialogue: —————————————

Audio: ———————

Scene:

Shot: Duration:

Description/Dialogue: —————————————

Audio: ———————

Scene:

Shot: Duration:

Description/Dialogue: —————————————

Audio: ———————

Scene:

Shot: Duration:

Description/Dialogue: —————————————

Audio: ———————

Scene:

Shot: Duration:

Description/Dialogue: —————————————

Audio: ———————

Scene:

Shot: Duration:

Description/Dialogue: _____

_____

Audio: _____

Scene:

Shot: Duration:

Description/Dialogue: _____

_____

Audio: _____

Scene:

Shot: Duration:

Description/Dialogue: _____

_____

Audio: _____

Scene:

Shot: Duration:

Description/Dialogue: _____

_____

Audio: _____

Scene:

Shot: Duration:

Description/Dialogue: _____

_____

Audio: _____

Scene:

Shot: Duration:

Description/Dialogue: _____

_____

Audio: _____

Scene:

Shot: Duration:

Description/Dialogue: _____

Audio: _____

Scene:

Shot: Duration:

Description/Dialogue: _____

Audio: _____

Scene:

Shot: Duration:

Description/Dialogue: _____

Audio: _____

Scene:

Shot: Duration:

Description/Dialogue: _____

Audio: _____

Scene:

Shot: Duration:

Description/Dialogue: _____

Audio: _____

Scene:

Shot: Duration:

Description/Dialogue: _____

Audio: _____

Scene:

Shot: Duration:

Description/Dialogue:

Audio:

Scene:

Shot: Duration:

Description/Dialogue:

Audio:

Scene:

Shot: Duration:

Description/Dialogue:

Audio:

Scene:

Shot: Duration:

Description/Dialogue:

Audio:

Scene:

Shot: Duration:

Description/Dialogue:

Audio:

Scene:

Shot: Duration:

Description/Dialogue:

Audio:

Scene:

Shot: Duration:

Description/Dialogue: _____

Audio: _____

Scene:

Shot: Duration:

Description/Dialogue: _____

Audio: _____

Scene:

Shot: Duration:

Description/Dialogue: _____

Audio: _____

Scene:

Shot: Duration:

Description/Dialogue: _____

Audio: _____

Scene:

Shot: Duration:

Description/Dialogue: _____

Audio: _____

Scene:

Shot: Duration:

Description/Dialogue: _____

Audio: _____

Scene:

Shot: Duration:

Description/Dialogue: _____

_____

Audio: _____

Scene:

Shot: Duration:

Description/Dialogue: _____

_____

Audio: _____

Scene:

Shot: Duration:

Description/Dialogue: _____

_____

Audio: _____

Scene:

Shot: Duration:

Description/Dialogue: _____

_____

Audio: _____

Scene:

Shot: Duration:

Description/Dialogue: _____

_____

Audio: _____

Scene:

Shot: Duration:

Description/Dialogue: _____

_____

Audio: _____

Scene:

Shot: Duration:

Description/Dialogue: _____

_____

Audio: _____

Scene:

Shot: Duration:

Description/Dialogue: _____

_____

Audio: _____

Scene:

Shot: Duration:

Description/Dialogue: _____

_____

Audio: _____

Scene:

Shot: Duration:

Description/Dialogue: _____

_____

Audio: _____

Scene:

Shot: Duration:

Description/Dialogue: _____

_____

Audio: _____

Scene:

Shot: Duration:

Description/Dialogue: _____

_____

Audio: _____

Scene:

Shot: Duration:

Description/Dialogue:

Audio:

Scene:

Shot: Duration:

Description/Dialogue:

Audio:

Scene:

Shot: Duration:

Description/Dialogue:

Audio:

Scene:

Shot: Duration:

Description/Dialogue:

Audio:

Scene:

Shot: Duration:

Description/Dialogue:

Audio:

Scene:

Shot: Duration:

Description/Dialogue:

Audio:

Scene:

Shot: Duration:

Description/Dialogue: _____

_____

Audio: _____

Scene:

Shot: Duration:

Description/Dialogue: _____

_____

Audio: _____

Scene:

Shot: Duration:

Description/Dialogue: _____

_____

Audio: _____

Scene:

Shot: Duration:

Description/Dialogue: _____

_____

Audio: _____

Scene:

Shot: Duration:

Description/Dialogue: _____

_____

Audio: _____

Scene:

Shot: Duration:

Description/Dialogue: _____

_____

Audio: _____

Scene:

Shot: Duration:

Description/Dialogue: _____

Audio: _____

Scene:

Shot: Duration:

Description/Dialogue: _____

Audio: _____

Scene:

Shot: Duration:

Description/Dialogue: _____

Audio: _____

Scene:

Shot: Duration:

Description/Dialogue: _____

Audio: _____

Scene:

Shot: Duration:

Description/Dialogue: _____

Audio: _____

Scene:

Shot: Duration:

Description/Dialogue: _____

Audio: _____

Scene:

Shot: Duration:

Description/Dialogue: _____

Audio: _____

Scene:

Shot: Duration:

Description/Dialogue: _____

Audio: _____

Scene:

Shot: Duration:

Description/Dialogue: _____

Audio: _____

Scene:

Shot: Duration:

Description/Dialogue: _____

Audio: _____

Scene:

Shot: Duration:

Description/Dialogue: _____

Audio: _____

Scene:

Shot: Duration:

Description/Dialogue: _____

Audio: _____

Scene:

Shot: Duration:

Description/Dialogue: _____

_____

Audio: _____

Scene:

Shot: Duration:

Description/Dialogue: _____

_____

Audio: _____

Scene:

Shot: Duration:

Description/Dialogue: _____

_____

Audio: _____

Scene:

Shot: Duration:

Description/Dialogue: _____

_____

Audio: _____

Scene:

Shot: Duration:

Description/Dialogue: _____

_____

Audio: _____

Scene:

Shot: Duration:

Description/Dialogue: _____

_____

Audio: _____

Scene:

Shot: Duration:

Description/Dialogue:

Audio:

Scene:

Shot: Duration:

Description/Dialogue:

Audio:

Scene:

Shot: Duration:

Description/Dialogue:

Audio:

Scene:

Shot: Duration:

Description/Dialogue:

Audio:

Scene:

Shot: Duration:

Description/Dialogue:

Audio:

Scene:

Shot: Duration:

Description/Dialogue:

Audio:

Scene:

Shot: Duration:

Description/Dialogue:

Audio:

Scene:

Shot: Duration:

Description/Dialogue:

Audio:

Scene:

Shot: Duration:

Description/Dialogue:

Audio:

Scene:

Shot: Duration:

Description/Dialogue:

Audio:

Scene:

Shot: Duration:

Description/Dialogue:

Audio:

Scene:

Shot: Duration:

Description/Dialogue:

Audio:

Scene:

Shot: Duration:

Description/Dialogue: —————————————

Audio: ————

Scene:

Shot: Duration:

Description/Dialogue: —————————————

Audio: ————

Scene:

Shot: Duration:

Description/Dialogue: —————————————

Audio: ————

Scene:

Shot: Duration:

Description/Dialogue: —————————————

Audio: ————

Scene:

Shot: Duration:

Description/Dialogue: —————————————

Audio: ————

Scene:

Shot: Duration:

Description/Dialogue: —————————————

Audio: ————

Scene:

Shot: Duration:

Description/Dialogue: _____

_____

Audio: _____

Scene:

Shot: Duration:

Description/Dialogue: _____

_____

Audio: _____

Scene:

Shot: Duration:

Description/Dialogue: _____

_____

Audio: _____

Scene:

Shot: Duration:

Description/Dialogue: _____

_____

Audio: _____

Scene:

Shot: Duration:

Description/Dialogue: _____

_____

Audio: _____

Scene:

Shot: Duration:

Description/Dialogue: _____

_____

Audio: _____

Scene:

Shot: Duration:

Description/Dialogue: _____

Audio: _____

Scene:

Shot: Duration:

Description/Dialogue: _____

Audio: _____

Scene:

Shot: Duration:

Description/Dialogue: _____

Audio: _____

Scene:

Shot: Duration:

Description/Dialogue: _____

Audio: _____

Scene:

Shot: Duration:

Description/Dialogue: _____

Audio: _____

Scene:

Shot: Duration:

Description/Dialogue: _____

Audio: _____

Scene:

Shot: Duration:

Description/Dialogue: _____

_____

Audio: _____

Scene:

Shot: Duration:

Description/Dialogue: _____

_____

Audio: _____

Scene:

Shot: Duration:

Description/Dialogue: _____

_____

Audio: _____

Scene:

Shot: Duration:

Description/Dialogue: _____

_____

Audio: _____

Scene:

Shot: Duration:

Description/Dialogue: _____

_____

Audio: _____

Scene:

Shot: Duration:

Description/Dialogue: _____

_____

Audio: _____

Scene:

Shot: | Duration:

Description/Dialogue: _____

Audio: _____

Scene:

Shot: | Duration:

Description/Dialogue: _____

Audio: _____

Scene:

Shot: | Duration:

Description/Dialogue: _____

Audio: _____

Scene:

Shot: | Duration:

Description/Dialogue: _____

Audio: _____

Scene:

Shot: | Duration:

Description/Dialogue: _____

Audio: _____

Scene:

Shot: | Duration:

Description/Dialogue: _____

Audio: _____

Scene:

Shot: Duration:

Description/Dialogue: _____

Audio: _____

Scene:

Shot: Duration:

Description/Dialogue: _____

Audio: _____

Scene:

Shot: Duration:

Description/Dialogue: _____

Audio: _____

Scene:

Shot: Duration:

Description/Dialogue: _____

Audio: _____

Scene:

Shot: Duration:

Description/Dialogue: _____

Audio: _____

Scene:

Shot: Duration:

Description/Dialogue: _____

Audio: _____

Scene:

Shot: Duration:

Description/Dialogue:

Audio:

Scene:

Shot: Duration:

Description/Dialogue:

Audio:

Scene:

Shot: Duration:

Description/Dialogue:

Audio:

Scene:

Shot: Duration:

Description/Dialogue:

Audio:

Scene:

Shot: Duration:

Description/Dialogue:

Audio:

Scene:

Shot: Duration:

Description/Dialogue:

Audio:

Scene:

Shot: Duration:

Description/Dialogue: _____

_____

Audio: _____

Scene:

Shot: Duration:

Description/Dialogue: _____

_____

Audio: _____

Scene:

Shot: Duration:

Description/Dialogue: _____

_____

Audio: _____

Scene:

Shot: Duration:

Description/Dialogue: _____

_____

Audio: _____

Scene:

Shot: Duration:

Description/Dialogue: _____

_____

Audio: _____

Scene:

Shot: Duration:

Description/Dialogue: _____

_____

Audio: _____

Scene:

Shot: Duration:

Description/Dialogue:

Audio:

Scene:

Shot: Duration:

Description/Dialogue:

Audio:

Scene:

Shot: Duration:

Description/Dialogue:

Audio:

Scene:

Shot: Duration:

Description/Dialogue:

Audio:

Scene:

Shot: Duration:

Description/Dialogue:

Audio:

Scene:

Shot: Duration:

Description/Dialogue:

Audio:

Scene:

Shot: Duration:

Description/Dialogue: _____

_____

Audio: _____

Scene:

Shot: Duration:

Description/Dialogue: _____

_____

Audio: _____

Scene:

Shot: Duration:

Description/Dialogue: _____

_____

Audio: _____

Scene:

Shot: Duration:

Description/Dialogue: _____

_____

Audio: _____

Scene:

Shot: Duration:

Description/Dialogue: _____

_____

Audio: _____

Scene:

Shot: Duration:

Description/Dialogue: _____

_____

Audio: _____

Scene:

Shot: Duration:

Description/Dialogue: _____

Audio: _____

Scene:

Shot: Duration:

Description/Dialogue: _____

Audio: _____

Scene:

Shot: Duration:

Description/Dialogue: _____

Audio: _____

Scene:

Shot: Duration:

Description/Dialogue: _____

Audio: _____

Scene:

Shot: Duration:

Description/Dialogue: _____

Audio: _____

Scene:

Shot: Duration:

Description/Dialogue: _____

Audio: _____

Scene:

Shot: Duration:

Description/Dialogue: _____

_____

_____

Audio: _____

Scene:

Shot: Duration:

Description/Dialogue: _____

_____

_____

Audio: _____

Scene:

Shot: Duration:

Description/Dialogue: _____

_____

_____

Audio: _____

Scene:

Shot: Duration:

Description/Dialogue: _____

_____

_____

Audio: _____

Scene:

Shot: Duration:

Description/Dialogue: _____

_____

_____

Audio: _____

Scene:

Shot: Duration:

Description/Dialogue: _____

_____

_____

Audio: _____

Scene:

Shot: Duration:

Description/Dialogue: _____

Audio: _____

Scene:

Shot: Duration:

Description/Dialogue: _____

Audio: _____

Scene:

Shot: Duration:

Description/Dialogue: _____

Audio: _____

Scene:

Shot: Duration:

Description/Dialogue: _____

Audio: _____

Scene:

Shot: Duration:

Description/Dialogue: _____

Audio: _____

Scene:

Shot: Duration:

Description/Dialogue: _____

Audio: _____

Scene:

Shot: Duration:

Description/Dialogue: _____

_____

Audio: _____

Scene:

Shot: Duration:

Description/Dialogue: _____

_____

Audio: _____

Scene:

Shot: Duration:

Description/Dialogue: _____

_____

Audio: _____

Scene:

Shot: Duration:

Description/Dialogue: _____

_____

Audio: _____

Scene:

Shot: Duration:

Description/Dialogue: _____

_____

Audio: _____

Scene:

Shot: Duration:

Description/Dialogue: _____

_____

Audio: _____

Scene:

Shot: Duration:

Description/Dialogue: _____

Audio: _____

Scene:

Shot: Duration:

Description/Dialogue: _____

Audio: _____

Scene:

Shot: Duration:

Description/Dialogue: _____

Audio: _____

Scene:

Shot: Duration:

Description/Dialogue: _____

Audio: _____

Scene:

Shot: Duration:

Description/Dialogue: _____

Audio: _____

Scene:

Shot: Duration:

Description/Dialogue: _____

Audio: _____

Scene:

Shot: Duration:

Description/Dialogue: _____

_____

Audio: _____

Scene:

Shot: Duration:

Description/Dialogue: _____

_____

Audio: _____

Scene:

Shot: Duration:

Description/Dialogue: _____

_____

Audio: _____

Scene:

Shot: Duration:

Description/Dialogue: _____

_____

Audio: _____

Scene:

Shot: Duration:

Description/Dialogue: _____

_____

Audio: _____

Scene:

Shot: Duration:

Description/Dialogue: _____

_____

Audio: _____

Scene:

Shot: Duration:

Description/Dialogue: _____

Audio: _____

Scene:

Shot: Duration:

Description/Dialogue: _____

Audio: _____

Scene:

Shot: Duration:

Description/Dialogue: _____

Audio: _____

Scene:

Shot: Duration:

Description/Dialogue: _____

Audio: _____

Scene:

Shot: Duration:

Description/Dialogue: _____

Audio: _____

Scene:

Shot: Duration:

Description/Dialogue: _____

Audio: _____

Scene:

Shot: _____ Duration: _____

Description/Dialogue: _____

_____

Audio: _____

Scene:

Shot: _____ Duration: _____

Description/Dialogue: _____

_____

Audio: _____

Scene:

Shot: _____ Duration: _____

Description/Dialogue: _____

_____

Audio: _____

Scene:

Shot: _____ Duration: _____

Description/Dialogue: _____

_____

Audio: _____

Scene:

Shot: _____ Duration: _____

Description/Dialogue: _____

_____

Audio: _____

Scene:

Shot: _____ Duration: _____

Description/Dialogue: _____

_____

Audio: _____

Scene:

Shot: Duration:

Description/Dialogue: _____

Audio: _____

Scene:

Shot: Duration:

Description/Dialogue: _____

Audio: _____

Scene:

Shot: Duration:

Description/Dialogue: _____

Audio: _____

Scene:

Shot: Duration:

Description/Dialogue: _____

Audio: _____

Scene:

Shot: Duration:

Description/Dialogue: _____

Audio: _____

Scene:

Shot: Duration:

Description/Dialogue: _____

Audio: _____

Scene:

Shot: Duration:

Description/Dialogue: _____

_____

Audio: _____

Scene:

Shot: Duration:

Description/Dialogue: _____

_____

Audio: _____

Scene:

Shot: Duration:

Description/Dialogue: _____

_____

Audio: _____

Scene:

Shot: Duration:

Description/Dialogue: _____

_____

Audio: _____

Scene:

Shot: Duration:

Description/Dialogue: _____

_____

Audio: _____

Scene:

Shot: Duration:

Description/Dialogue: _____

_____

Audio: _____

Scene:

Shot: Duration:

Description/Dialogue: _____

Audio: _____

Scene:

Shot: Duration:

Description/Dialogue: _____

Audio: _____

Scene:

Shot: Duration:

Description/Dialogue: _____

Audio: _____

Scene:

Shot: Duration:

Description/Dialogue: _____

Audio: _____

Scene:

Shot: Duration:

Description/Dialogue: _____

Audio: _____

Scene:

Shot: Duration:

Description/Dialogue: _____

Audio: _____

Scene:

Shot: Duration:

Description/Dialogue: _____

Audio: _____

Scene:

Shot: Duration:

Description/Dialogue: _____

Audio: _____

Scene:

Shot: Duration:

Description/Dialogue: _____

Audio: _____

Scene:

Shot: Duration:

Description/Dialogue: _____

Audio: _____

Scene:

Shot: Duration:

Description/Dialogue: _____

Audio: _____

Scene:

Shot: Duration:

Description/Dialogue: _____

Audio: _____

Scene:

Shot: Duration:

Description/Dialogue: _____

_____

Audio: _____

Scene:

Shot: Duration:

Description/Dialogue: _____

_____

Audio: _____

Scene:

Shot: Duration:

Description/Dialogue: _____

_____

Audio: _____

Scene:

Shot: Duration:

Description/Dialogue: _____

_____

Audio: _____

Scene:

Shot: Duration:

Description/Dialogue: _____

_____

Audio: _____

Scene:

Shot: Duration:

Description/Dialogue: _____

_____

Audio: _____

Scene:

Shot: Duration:

Description/Dialogue:

Audio:

Scene:

Shot: Duration:

Description/Dialogue:

Audio:

Scene:

Shot: Duration:

Description/Dialogue:

Audio:

Scene:

Shot: Duration:

Description/Dialogue:

Audio:

Scene:

Shot: Duration:

Description/Dialogue:

Audio:

Scene:

Shot: Duration:

Description/Dialogue:

Audio:

Scene:

Shot: Duration:

Description/Dialogue:

Audio:

Scene:

Shot: Duration:

Description/Dialogue:

Audio:

Scene:

Shot: Duration:

Description/Dialogue:

Audio:

Scene:

Shot: Duration:

Description/Dialogue:

Audio:

Scene:

Shot: Duration:

Description/Dialogue:

Audio:

Scene:

Shot: Duration:

Description/Dialogue:

Audio:

Made in the USA
Middletown, DE
18 December 2020